Lecture Notes in Economics and Mathematical Systems

498

Springer-Verlag Berlin Heidelberg GmbH

Michael Reutter

A Macroeconomic Model of West German Unemployment

Theory and Evidence

Springer

Author

Dr. Michael Reutter
Center for Economic Studies (CES)
University of Munich
Schackstraße 4
80539 Munich, Germany

Cataloging-in-Publication data applied for

Die Deutsche Bibliothek - CIP-Einheitsaufnahme

Reutter, Michael:
A macroeconomic model of west German unemployment : theory and evidence / Michael Reutter. - Berlin ; Heidelberg ; New York ; Barcelona ; Hong Kong ; London ; Milan ; Paris ; Singapore ; Tokyo : Springer, 2001
(Lecture notes in economics and mathematical systems ; 498)
ISBN 978-3-540-41244-1   ISBN 978-3-642-18159-7 (eBook)
DOI 10.1007/978-3-642-18159-7

ISSN 0075-8450
ISBN 978-3-540-41244-1

"Gedruckt mit Unterstützung der Deutschen Forschungsgemeinschaft D 019"

Typesetting: Camera ready by author
Printed on acid-free paper   SPIN: 10786747   55/3142/du   5 4 3 2 1 0

Preface

This book was accepted in 1999 as doctoral thesis (Dr. oec. publ.) by the faculty of economics of the Ludwig-Maximilians-Universität in Munich. It won the dissertation price of the Alumni-Club of the economics faculty in the academic year 2000. Financial assistance by the German Research Association (DFG) for printing costs is gratefully acknowledged. I have to thank the people behind the LaTeX-project, in particular Donald Knuth and Leslie Lamport, for their wonderful typesetting program.

The supervisors of my thesis were Prof. Dr. G. Flaig and Prof. Dr. D. Marin. I would like thank both for their thorough reading of the book and their ideas and critical remarks. I owe much gratitude to my academic teacher Prof. Dr. G. Flaig for many insightful conversations about modern time series econometrics, asymptotic theory and data problems. His emphasis on clear theory combined with sound econometric methods formed my personal ideal of how to do applied economics. After he left the university in 1998 I had the opportunity to continue my work at the Center for Economic Studies. Prof. Dr. H.-W. Sinn and my new colleagues at CES provided a stimulating environment for the completion of my dissertation. Finally, I want to thank my parents, my sister and my friends for being there and sharing my cheers and worries.

Munich, October 2000 *Michael Reutter*

Our main concern in philosophy and in science should be the search for truth. Justification is not an aim; and brilliance and cleverness as such are boring. We should seek to see or discover the most urgent problems, and we should try to solve them by proposing true theories (or true statements, or true propositions; there is no need here to distinguish between these); or at any rate by proposing theories which come a little nearer to the truth than those of our predecessors.

Popper, Karl-Raimund
Objective Knowledge: An Evolutionary Approach, 1972

Contents

1. Introduction

Today, involuntary unemployment poses the major economic problem in many European countries. Despite great efforts, the economic profession is not able to give clear advice to policy-makers on how to solve the dilemma. However, the necessary measures are often less controversial than the casual observer might think. At least in Germany there seems to be a consensus among most economists that the appropriate instruments are supply-side measures aimed at reducing labour costs and not the demand-side policies as advocated for example by the former German minister of finance Oskar Lafontaine.[1] High on the agenda is a reduction in real wages that should help to spur labour demand. This seems to reflect the assessment that the major part of German unemployment is of a structural type.

If real wages are too high, the task of the economist is to explain what factors have led to this result and how the real wage can be influenced by the instruments that are available to the government. There has been great progress on the theoretical side of the issue and today we are faced not with too few, but rather with too many possible explanations of this phenomenon, at least from the viewpoint of a policy-maker. As in every other science, such a plethora of theories has triggered empirical studies aimed at discriminating between the suggested explanations. Unfortunately, a clear picture has not yet emerged.[2] This book is an attempt to make progress on the subject with a structural econometric model of the employment rate that delivers a convincing explanation of the West German labour market experience in the last thirty years.

There are two major aspects of the work presented here that are of particular interest. The first one is related to the discrimination between cyclical and long-run developments and the evaluation of their respective importance in explaining unemployment in West Germany. In figure 1.1 the unemploy-

[1] This was the result of a survey among economists carried out by Stefan Profit and Rolf Tschernig on two conferences at the Humboldt University in Berlin Profit and Tschernig (1998).

[2] This is the impression given by the survey of macroeconomic explanations of unemployment and their empirical relevance by Manning (1995a).

ment rates of the United States u_{US} and West Germany[3] u_G are plotted for the period from 1959 to 1996.

Fig. 1.1. Unemployment rates for the US and West Germany

The graph shows that both economies were hit by similar shocks that induced cycles in the unemployment series. However, while in the US the unemployment rate reverted to its pre-shock level, the German unemployment series seems to display shock persistence, meaning that the shocks have had a permanent effect on the long-run level of unemployment—or the "natural" rate of unemployment as it is called (Friedman, 1968). Although this is a popular interpretation, there is another possible view of the series. The picture could also be interpreted as an unemployment rate that fluctuates around an increasing trend. The shocks are temporary and do not affect the long-run level of unemployment; the trend is caused by exogenous factors that have led to an increase in the natural rate. This view was challenged in the eighties and early nineties, because the main suspects for such a development had not increased enough or even decreased in the eighties in many countries, while unemployment rose to unprecedented levels.[4] One of the innovations of the model presented later is the introduction of a new factor that has not yet been considered important and that could help to solve the puzzle. This new factor is capital income taxation, which leads to the second point.

[3] To assure comparability, the series for Germany is not the official unemployment rate, but an approximation of the US concept published by the US Bureau of Labor Statistics.

[4] See Manning (1995a) for a summary of the arguments for the UK.

An important issue that has generally not been given enough weight in the discussion on wage determination is distributional fairness. While the impact on wages and employment of an increasing burden on labour income through wage taxes and social insurance contributions has long been recognized, the decrease in the effective tax rates on capital income has not received the same attention. An obvious explanation for this fact is that less source-based capital taxation in an open economy with mobile capital generally means more rather than less employment, because the net return on capital increases, in equilibrium the capital stock is higher, and for any given real wage employment is higher as well.

The picture that emerges from the analysis in this book is quite different. The argument here is that changes in the capital stock should be neutral towards employment in the long-run, because wages finally adapt to changes in productivity. On the other hand, wage setting might be non-neutral towards the decrease in capital income taxation because of fairness considerations. In a union-firm bargaining framework, a model that seems to be especially important for Germany, this conforms to a view of "fair shares" that is discussed in the seminal article by McDonald and Solow (1981). This view has not played an important role in the literature so far. The reason for this is quite simple: the Nash bargaining model (Nash, 1950) that is applied almost exclusively to wage bargaining neglects these fairness considerations. In the traditional specification of the model, the interesting variable in this respect is not the capital income tax but the tax on pure profit. As noted by de Menil (1971), a proportional profit tax is neutral towards employment in the wage bargaining model with the Nash solution. The same holds for the capital income tax with a different specification of the model developed later in the book. This result could be an explanation of why the discussion concerning the relevance of the profit tax in a Phillips curve framework (Perry, 1966) was not continued in the bargaining literature. It seems that many economists have problems with models that imply interpersonal utility comparisons, as most models of fairness do. The simple reason may be that a cardinal "utility" is a somewhat elusive concept that is best avoided and of course can be avoided in most circumstances. Whether it is reasonable to ignore such interpersonal utility comparisons in cooperative bargaining models is questionable, however. There are many empirical studies giving evidence that this is not justified (for a survey see Roth and Malouf, 1979) and, as will be argued in this book, it might play a considerable role in wage negotiations, as well. If this is true, a decrease in capital income taxation that is not accompanied by an offsetting decrease in wage taxation might under fairness considerations lead to a compensation of the employed in the form of higher wages and thereby higher unemployment.

The potential importance of this argument for European unemployment is shown in figure 1.2. The figure shows that in Europe the eighties and the nineties were a period of a considerable shift of the tax burden towards

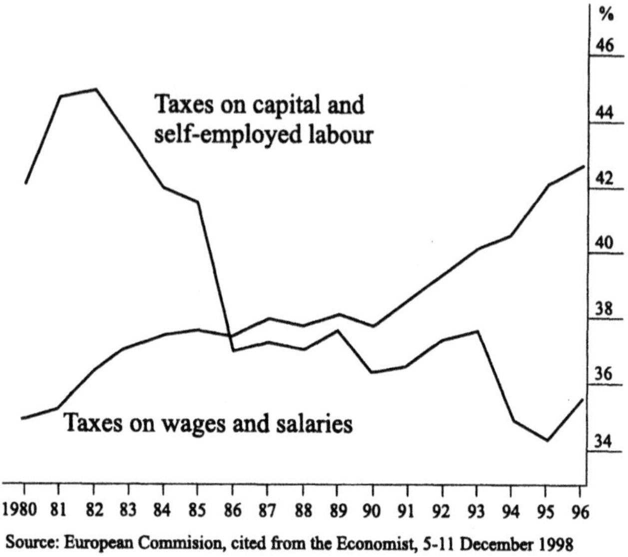

Fig. 1.2. Average tax rates on capital and wages in Europe

employed labour. This development is well known to the trade unions and employers associations. It seems not unreasonable that strong trade unions try to shift the burden back in the form of higher wages. This possibility is explored from a theoretical as well as from an empirical perspective in this book, and the results from this analysis constitute its main contribution to the ongoing debate.

In the rest of this introductory chapter, a short overview and the main results of the book will be presented. In chapter 2 the econometric concepts that are of relevance for the empirical part of the book are introduced. Since the time series used in this part are nonstationary, the appropriate econometric tool to conduct empirical research is cointegration analysis. There exists a large literature on the subject now and it is difficult to keep track of every development in the field. Since the cointegration methods used are not standard, it seems necessary to explain them in a separate section and to discuss the importance of this deviation from classical textbook econometrics using OLS. A second point that deserves attention when doing time series analysis is seasonality. This feature of most macroeconomic time series has been given much attention in the literature in the past decade. Today, it is no longer seen as innocuous to use seasonally adjusted data even in a study of long-run relations, and therefore a second section serves the purpose of giving a short introduction to the field, stressing the different testing procedures for seasonal integration that have been developed.

Chapter 3 gives a short overview of the development of trade union theory, from the first attempts in the middle of the century to the early eighties. In the first section the standard forms of the most important wage bargaining models that have been developed are discussed. The main purpose is to define concepts and introduce language. In the second section the existing empirical studies using modern time series methods are compared with respect to a few important points, and the differences to the approach of this book are emphasized.

Chapter 4 focuses on the bargaining solution that is applied to union-firm wage negotiations. As mentioned above, the issue of fairness and its relation to axioms of proposed bargaining solutions is at the center of the discussion here. The generally used Nash solution is compared to the proportional solution, which is the alternative model that is used in the empirical part of the book. This solution has not been used very often in the literature and, therefore, a thorough analysis of the pros and cons of this solution is necessary to justify its use. As is shown in this chapter, the proportional solution overcomes several shortcomings of the Nash solution that are important in the union-firm context. The major difference concerns the comparative statics of the solutions. Only with the proportional solution do taxes that simply scale the utility of one of the bargaining parties have an influence on the bargaining outcome. If the bargain is over wages only, as is generally the case in Germany, the wage is influenced by such taxes in a simple and intuitive way under the proportional solution but is not affected under the Nash solution. The switch to the proportional solution therefore introduces a new factor in wage and employment equations: the capital income tax mentioned above.

Although the wage bargaining model seems to be the natural choice to model wage determination in Germany, there are other theories of involuntary unemployment that cannot easily be dismissed as explanations. The most popular alternative is efficiency wage theory. In chapter 5 I try to discriminate between these two models on the basis of the dynamic interaction between actual and contract wages. There is a simple intuition for this approach. In an economy where the efficiency wage is the driving force behind wage changes, one should observe that contract wages can be forecast by lagged actual wages, because changes in the efficiency wage should be first reflected in actual wages and only after a time lag in contract wages. This is because contract wages are negotiated only once a year, while the typical firm has several rounds of wage adjustment during the year. If, in contrast, contract wages are the driving force, then the typical firm does not have an incentive to change wages during the year and will passively let wages adjust according to wage agreements. Of course, there are caveats against this argument, and these are discussed in the chapter as well. The main result that emerges from the causality analysis is that at least since the early seventies efficiency wage theory is unlikely to be the appropriate model for explaining the growth in actual wages in West Germany.

With this confirming result, in chapter 6 an economic and econometric model of wage setting and employment, based on the bargaining framework, is developed. While the comparative statics are quite simple, it is interesting to see that it is possible to have loglinear wage and employment equations under plausible assumptions about technology and preferences. The model that is developed uses a Cobb-Douglas technology and a union utility that is a simpler version of the general class of utilities introduced by Manning (1993). The intention is to construct a model of the long-run behaviour of wages and employment. Therefore, it is important that the chosen specification leads to a long-run neutrality of employment with respect to technology and the capital stock.

In chapter 7 the econometric methods introduced in chapter 2 are applied to test for a long-run relation between the employment rate and the variables identified as important in chapter 6. After an explanation of the data used in the study, the seasonal structure is analyzed and the appropriate seasonal filters are determined. Using the seasonally adjusted series, it is shown that the derived equation for the equilibrium employment rate is a cointegration relation, and the parameters are estimated. The signs of the parameters are in accordance with the predictions of the theoretical model, and a stability analysis is conducted. Taken together, the result is that the model is able to explain the evolution of unemployment in West Germany over the last thirty years with only three variables. This is a considerable achievement for such a simple model. The important factors are the ratio of producer and consumer prices, the so-called tax wedge (comprising labour taxes and social insurance contributions), and the capital income tax. The negative influence of the reduction in capital income taxation on employment is confirmed by the empirical evidence.

Having identified the main trending variables that deliver a model of the natural rate in West Germany, the question remains whether shocks to unemployment have had significant repercussions on these variables. This is generally discussed under the heading of "hysteresis" effect and is investigated in chapter 8. The idea is that a shock to unemployment, like the oil price shocks in the seventies, led to a permanent change in the long-run determinants of unemployment. The variables generally mentioned are trade union membership, long-term unemployment, and the capital stock. After the shock, unemployment does not return to its pre-shock level, because the natural rate has increased. Often, these variables are not explicitly included in the empirical estimation. Therefore, it is not possible to identify whether the effect is really caused by the shock feeding back to the trend or by an exogenous increase in the trend. For such an analysis, a fully specified model of the natural rate as developed in this book is quite useful, since it identifies the important trending variables and permits a direct exogeneity test. The variables that play a role in the model of chapter 7 are quite different, though, from the variables mentioned above. However, one could imagine that there is a feedback from higher unemployment on social insurance contributions through an increase in the contribution rate for unemployment insurance.

The analysis in this chapter shows that there is only weak evidence for such an effect in West Germany.

In chapter 9 the policy implications of these results are derived. The aim is to make recommendations for political reform and evaluate several proposals to reduce unemployment that have been put forward by German politicians.

2. Econometric Methods

In the last decade there has been a rapid development in the field of econometric models for nonstationary data that allow for a distinction between short-run dynamics and long-run relationships. While this distinction can be made in dynamic models with stationary variables as well, it is much more powerful in nonstationary models. In the stationary case, the existence of a long-run relation is a necessary implication of the validity of the dynamic model. Therefore, the task is simply to calculate the long-run multipliers from the short-run parameters. In models with nonstationary variables, however, the existence of a long-run relation is a mere possibility, called "cointegration". When economic models state such relations, a cointegration test amounts to a test of the model itself. Significance and correct sign of the parameters in the estimation of the model is no longer sufficient to support the underlying theory. With nonstationary data the criterion is stricter, since cointegration requires a very good "fit" of the model in a certain sense. The reason for this additional requirement is the observation that nonstationary time series tend to produce positive correlations even when they are independent processes. This is discussed in the literature as "spurious regression"; it can be dated back to Yule (1926) and was further investigated by Granger and Newbold (1974) and Phillips (1986).

For the statistical representation of these models for nonstationary data, different approaches have been suggested. It has to be decided whether only an estimate the long-run relation is required or whether the short-run dynamics should be modeled as well. In the first case, it is sufficient to model the long-run relation and the short-run is captured by the error process. In the second case, one possibility is to adopt a closed model in which the distribution of all variables is specified. The most popular way to do this is in form of a Gaussian vector autoregressive model (VAR). This framework is the basis of the approach put forward by Johansen (1988). Alternatively, an open model with exogenous variables can be employed, where only the conditional distribution of a subset of variables is modeled. Proponents of this approach include Hendry (1995) and Boswijk (1992).

The analysis in this book focuses on the long-run relation between the employment rate and a set of explanatory variables in chapter 7. But short-run dynamics play an important role as well. In chapter 8 the interaction between the variables in the long-run relation is analyzed and in chapter 5 the dynamic correlations between wage variables is examined. Since the methods used for these purposes are not the same and not always standard, section 2.1 gives a short introduction to the main concepts. The first part of the discussion concentrates on an estimation method for the cointegration vector neglecting the short-run dynamics. The second part shows how the short-run dynamics can be modeled together with the long-run relation.

A second issue that plays a considerable role in modern time series analysis is the correct way of treating seasonality in the data (see Franses, 1996, for a survey). Since I always use quarterly data, this feature of the data is pervasive in the models. The main point here is the question of whether it is possible to separate a seasonal and a nonseasonal component in a time series, allowing a seasonal adjustment of the data. In the statistical models generally used to describe a changing seasonal pattern this is not possible, in contrast to the dummy variable model with deterministic seasonality, for example. The methods to discriminate between different forms of seasonality and the appropriate treatment of it are discussed in section 2.2.

2.1 Cointegration Analysis

In this section models and estimation procedures for nonstationary data are introduced. It is not intended to give a survey of the literature (for this see Hamilton, 1994); the focus is on the discussion of methods that are actually used in the book and that are not already standard in the literature.

The nonstationarity that is considered here is of a particular form in all the models and by now a whole branch of econometrics is named after this special form: "unit root econometrics". The meaning of this name is best explained with a simple autoregressive model of a univariate time series x_t as given by

$$\phi(L)x_t = \epsilon_t \;, \tag{2.1}$$

where $\phi(L) = 1 - \phi_1 L - \cdots - \phi_p L^p$ is a polynomial in the lag operator L and ϵ_t is white noise. In the same manner as for a difference equation, it is possible to tell something about the long-run behaviour of the series for given parameters ϕ_i. If the factorization of the polynomial

$$1 - \phi_1 L - \cdots - \phi_p L^p = (1 - \lambda_1 L)(1 - \lambda_2 L) \ldots (1 - \lambda_p L) \tag{2.2}$$

leads to roots λ_i inside the unit circle, then the difference equation is stable and the associated autoregressive process is (weakly) stationary, i.e. the mean is constant, the variance is constant, and the covariance between two x_t at different time periods depends solely on the distance between the two.

If one of the roots is on the unit circle, however, we speak of a unit root process or (first order) integrated process. The simplest example is a random walk

$$x_t = x_{t-1} + \epsilon_t \ , \tag{2.3}$$

which has a fundamentally different long-run behaviour than a stationary process. Through recursive substitution it is possible to rewrite the process as

$$x_t = x_0 + \sum_{i=1}^{t} \epsilon_i \ , \tag{2.4}$$

and conditional on x_0, the variance of the process is determined by the sum of the error terms. A simple calculation shows that the variance of the process increases with t, and for $t \to \infty$ the variance approaches infinity as well. Such a behaviour is called a stochastic trend, and the most widely used test for the existence of such a stochastic trend has been presented by Dickey and Fuller (1979). The simple idea is to estimate the autoregression and test for a unit coefficient on the lagged dependent variable. If the series shows a visible trend, then a linear time trend is included in the regression because a stationary model would not be a reasonable alternative. In most applications of the test, lagged first differences of the dependent variable are also included to account for additional autocorrelation in the series and this test is called "augmented Dickey-Fuller test" (ADF test). Beginning with Nelson and Plosser (1982), many studies have applied this test to macroeconomic time series and have shown that a stochastic trend can be found in many of these series, often in addition to a deterministic linear trend. An important feature of the test is the nonstandard distribution of the test statistic under the null hypothesis of a unit root, the so-called Dickey-Fuller distribution.[1] This behaviour of statistics is pervasive in unit root econometrics and one of the reasons for the large number of new estimation and testing procedures. The existence of unit roots is not a mere nuisance, however; it also leads to interesting new relations between statistical models and economic theory.

If a stochastic trend is present in the data, classic textbook econometrics are generally not valid anymore when relations between these variables are analyzed. As noted above, the parameter in a regression of two time series that contain stochastic trends does not converge to zero when the number of observations approaches infinity even when the processes are independent random walks. An important step in the development of proper estimation procedures has been the paper by Engle and Granger (1987), where it is shown that in a multivariate framework a linear combination of variables containing a stochastic trend can be stationary. If such a relation exists, the

[1] For small sample simulations and estimated response surfaces for the ADF test, see MacKinnon (1994).

variables are cointegrated. The intuition is that the variables share a common stochastic trend tying the variables together in the long-run. Often we would interpret economic theory as implying exactly this property. While deviations from an equilibrium are possible in the short-run, the forces of the market will restore the equilibrium in the long-run. If the variables in the economic model are best described with unit root processes, the existence of such a cointegration relation has become the natural way to put the model to a first test even before any parameters are estimated.

After this informal introduction, some aspects of these models will be discussed in more detail. The starting point of the discussion will be the following triangular representation of a cointegrated system used by Phillips (1991):

$$y_t = \boldsymbol{\beta}'\mathbf{x}_t + u_{1t} \tag{2.5}$$

$$\Delta\mathbf{x}_t = \mathbf{u}_{2t} \,, \tag{2.6}$$

where $\mathbf{u}_t' = (u_{1t}, \mathbf{u}_{2t}')$ is a vector stochastic process of dimension n. The first equation represents the cointegration relation with cointegration vector $(1, -\boldsymbol{\beta}')$. The error process is assumed to be stationary with zero mean, finite covariance matrix

$$\boldsymbol{\Pi} = \begin{bmatrix} \pi_{11} & \boldsymbol{\pi}_{21}' \\ \boldsymbol{\pi}_{21} & \boldsymbol{\Pi}_{22} \end{bmatrix} , \tag{2.7}$$

continuous spectral density matrix $f_{uu}(\xi)$ and long-run covariance matrix

$$2\pi f_{uu}(0) = \boldsymbol{\Omega} = \begin{bmatrix} \omega_{11} & \boldsymbol{\omega}_{21}' \\ \boldsymbol{\omega}_{21} & \boldsymbol{\Omega}_{22} \end{bmatrix} = \boldsymbol{\Pi} + \boldsymbol{\Lambda} + \boldsymbol{\Lambda}' \tag{2.8}$$

$$\boldsymbol{\Lambda} = \begin{bmatrix} \lambda_{11} & \boldsymbol{\lambda}_{21}' \\ \boldsymbol{\lambda}_{21} & \boldsymbol{\Lambda}_{22} \end{bmatrix} = \sum_{s=1}^{\infty} E(\mathbf{u}_t \mathbf{u}_{t+s}') \,, \tag{2.9}$$

which has an important role in the derivation of the asymptotic theory. Further, it is assumed that $\mathbf{u}_t$ satisfies the multivariate invariance principle

$$T^{-1/2} \sum_{j=1}^{[Tr]} \mathbf{u}_j \Rightarrow \mathbf{B}(r) \equiv \mathbf{BM}(\boldsymbol{\Omega}), \qquad 0 < r \leq 1 \,, \tag{2.10}$$

where [ ] denotes the integer part, $\Rightarrow$ is weak convergence and $\mathbf{BM}(\boldsymbol{\Omega})$ is vector Brownian motion with covariance matrix $\boldsymbol{\Omega}$. Conditions on $\mathbf{u}_t$ for this to hold are given by Phillips and Durlauf (1986). For an integrated process $\mathbf{p}_t$ constructed from $\mathbf{u}_t$ by

$$\mathbf{p}_t = \mathbf{p}_{t-1} + \mathbf{u}_t \qquad \mathbf{p}_0 = 0 \tag{2.11}$$

the following holds (Park and Phillips, 1988, 1989):

$$T^{-2}\sum_{t=1}^{T}\mathbf{p}_t\mathbf{p}_t' \Rightarrow \int_0^1 \mathbf{B}(r)\mathbf{B}(r)'dr \tag{2.12}$$

$$T^{-1}\sum_{t=1}^{T}\mathbf{p}_t\mathbf{u}_t' \Rightarrow \int_0^1 \mathbf{B}(r)d\mathbf{B}(r)' + \boldsymbol{\Pi} + \boldsymbol{\Lambda}\,. \tag{2.13}$$

For the estimation of $\boldsymbol{\beta}$ there are several methods available; the properties of each are given below. First, one can estimate by OLS. This was proposed by Engle and Granger (1987) and is known to be superconsistent, i.e. the estimator converges to the true value faster than the OLS estimator in the classic regression model with stationary variables. The asymptotic distribution of the OLS estimator depends on the specification of the error process. If the error process is i.i.d. with covariance matrix

$$\boldsymbol{\Pi} = \begin{bmatrix} \pi_{11} & \mathbf{0}' \\ \mathbf{0} & \boldsymbol{\Pi}_{22} \end{bmatrix}, \tag{2.14}$$

then u_{1t} and $\mathbf{u}_{2t}$ are incoherent, i.e. uncorrelated at all lags, which amounts to strict exogeneity of $\mathbf{x}_t$ in (2.5). In this case the OLS estimator is asymptotically distributed as

$$T(\hat{\boldsymbol{\beta}} - \boldsymbol{\beta}) = \left(T^{-2}\sum_{t=1}^{T}\mathbf{x}_t\mathbf{x}_t'\right)^{-1}\left(T^{-1}\sum_{t=1}^{T}\mathbf{x}_t u_{1t}\right) \tag{2.15}$$

$$\Rightarrow \left(\int_0^1 \mathbf{B}_2\mathbf{B}_2'\right)^{-1}\left(\int_0^1 \mathbf{B}_2 dB_1\right), \tag{2.16}$$

where

$$\begin{bmatrix} B_1(r) \\ \mathbf{B}_2(r) \end{bmatrix}_{n-1}^{1} = \mathbf{BM}(\boldsymbol{\Pi}) \tag{2.17}$$

is partitioned conformably with $\mathbf{u}_t$. Therefore, B_1 and $\mathbf{B}_2$ are independent. For testing it is important that in this case the estimator is normally distributed conditional on $\mathbf{B}_2$:

$$\left(\int_0^1 \mathbf{B}_2\mathbf{B}_2'\right)^{-1}\left(\int_0^1 \mathbf{B}_2 dB_1\right)\Bigg|_{\mathbf{B}_2} \equiv N\left(0, \pi_{11}\left(\int_0^1 \mathbf{B}_2\mathbf{B}_2'\right)^{-1}\right). \tag{2.18}$$

This leads to the standard χ^2 distribution of the associated Wald statistic. From the conditional distribution one can integrate to obtain the following representation as a covariance mixture of normals:

$$T(\hat{\boldsymbol{\beta}} - \boldsymbol{\beta}) \Rightarrow \int_{\mathbf{G}>0} N(0, \pi_{11}\mathbf{G})dP(\mathbf{G}), \quad \mathbf{G} = \left(\int_0^1 \mathbf{B}_2\mathbf{B}_2'\right)^{-1}, \tag{2.19}$$

where P is the probability measure associated with $\mathbf{G}$. In the general case, without restrictions on the correlation of the error process, there is a bias in the limiting distribution of $\hat{\beta}$:

$$T(\hat{\beta} - \beta) \Rightarrow \left(\int_0^1 \mathbf{B}_2 \mathbf{B}_2' \right)^{-1} \left(\int_0^1 \mathbf{B}_2 dB_1 + \boldsymbol{\pi}_{21} + \boldsymbol{\lambda}_{21} \right) , \tag{2.20}$$

where

$$\begin{bmatrix} B_1(r) \\ \mathbf{B}_2(r) \end{bmatrix}_{n-1}^{1} = \mathbf{BM}(\boldsymbol{\Omega}) . \tag{2.21}$$

Generally, the Brownian motion is correlated and the conditional distribution is not normal. Because the superconsistency is not affected, this is called "asymptotic second order bias". This is quite interesting, since in the case of a stationary regression the consistency of the OLS estimator would break down if u_{1t} is contemporaneously correlated with $\mathbf{u}_{2t}$.

However, as was shown in Monte Carlo studies (Banerjee et al., 1986), despite the superconsistency, the asymptotic second order bias can lead to biased estimates in small samples. Several cures have been proposed, among them the estimator of Saikkonen (1991) and Phillips and Loretan (1991) that includes leads and lags of the first differences of $\mathbf{x}_t$ in the OLS estimation, or the "fully modified estimator" (FM-OLS) of Phillips and Hansen (1990) that makes a nonparametric correction for the correlation. In chapter 7 the FM-OLS estimator is used to estimate the long-run relation, because there are also a number of stability tests based on this estimation procedure developed by Hansen (1992).

The idea behind the FM-OLS estimator is to correct the OLS estimator using an estimate of the long-run covariance matrix $\boldsymbol{\Omega}$ in such a way that the bias vanishes. The long-run covariance matrix can be estimated from the OLS residuals using the kernel estimator suggested by Newey and West (1987):

$$\hat{\boldsymbol{\Omega}} = \sum_{k=-m}^{m} w\left(\frac{k}{m}\right) \frac{1}{T} \sum_t \hat{\mathbf{u}}_{t+k} \hat{\mathbf{u}}_t' , \tag{2.22}$$

where w(.) is any kernel that produces positive semidefinite covariance estimates. It can be shown that in the transformed regression

$$y_t^+ = \beta' \mathbf{x}_t + u_{1t}^+ \tag{2.23}$$

$$y_t^+ = y_t - \hat{\boldsymbol{\omega}}_{21}' (\hat{\boldsymbol{\Omega}}_{22})^{-1} \Delta \mathbf{x}_t \tag{2.24}$$

$$u_{1t}^+ = u_{1t} - \hat{\boldsymbol{\omega}}_{21}' (\hat{\boldsymbol{\Omega}}_{22})^{-1} \Delta \mathbf{x}_t \tag{2.25}$$

the Brownian motion $\mathbf{B}^+$ in the asymptotic distribution of the OLS estimate of β is not correlated any more. What is then left to do is to adjust $\sum_{t=1}^{T} \mathbf{x}_t y_t^+$ for an estimate of the term $\boldsymbol{\pi}_{21}^+ + \boldsymbol{\lambda}_{21}^+$ corresponding to the vector $(u_{1t}^+, \mathbf{u}_{2t})$.

This term can also be estimated from the OLS residuals of the first regression, leading to the following asymptotic distribution of the FM-OLS estimator:

$$\begin{aligned} T(\hat{\beta}_{FM} - \beta) &= \left(T^{-2}\sum_{t=1}^{T} \mathbf{x}_t\mathbf{x}_t'\right)^{-1} \left(T^{-1}\sum_{t=1}^{T} \mathbf{x}_t u_{1t}^+ - \hat{\pi}_{21}^+ - \hat{\lambda}_{21}^+\right) \\ &\Rightarrow \left(\int_0^1 \mathbf{B}_2^+\mathbf{B}_2^{+'}\right)^{-1} \left(\int_0^1 \mathbf{B}_2^+ dB_1^+\right) . \end{aligned} \tag{2.26}$$

The FM-OLS estimator is asymptotically unbiased and leads to asymptotically χ^2 distributed Wald statistics.

A different starting point for the discussion of cointegration and estimation is given by the framework of a Gaussian VAR defined for the vector $\mathbf{z}_t' = (y_t, \mathbf{x}_t')$ used by Johansen (1988):

$$\boldsymbol{\Phi}(L)\mathbf{z}_t = \boldsymbol{\epsilon}_t \tag{2.27}$$

$$\boldsymbol{\Phi}(L) = \mathbf{I} - \boldsymbol{\Phi}_1 L - \boldsymbol{\Phi}_2 L^2 - \cdots - \boldsymbol{\Phi}_p L^p , \tag{2.28}$$

where the $\boldsymbol{\epsilon}_t$ are n.i.i.d. with mean zero and covariance matrix $\boldsymbol{\Omega}$. This model can be seen as an unrestricted reduced form of a dynamic model where all variables are endogenous. The matrix lag polynomial $\boldsymbol{\Phi}(L)$ can have unit roots like in the univariate case, and it is assumed that the first difference of $\mathbf{z}_t$ is a stationary vector process. As shown by Engle and Granger (1987) the existence of cointegration between the $\mathbf{z}_t$ variables has several important implications for the VAR representation. A reparameterization of the model leads to the following representation of the VAR called error correction model (ECM):

$$\Delta\mathbf{z}_t = \boldsymbol{\Pi}\mathbf{z}_{t-1} + \mathbf{A}_1\Delta\mathbf{z}_{t-1} + \cdots + \mathbf{A}_{p-1}\Delta\mathbf{z}_{t-p+1} + \boldsymbol{\epsilon}_t , \tag{2.29}$$

where $\boldsymbol{\Pi}$ and the $\mathbf{A}_i$ are functions of the $\boldsymbol{\Phi}_i$. The interesting case is when the matrix $\boldsymbol{\Pi}$ is a reduced rank matrix that can be written as $\boldsymbol{\alpha\gamma}'$. The matrix $\boldsymbol{\alpha}$ and the matrix $\boldsymbol{\gamma}$ are of dimension $n \times r$, where r is the rank of the matrix $\boldsymbol{\Pi}$. If the rank of the matrix is zero, then the VAR can be written as a VAR in first differences and there is no cointegration. If the rank is between zero and n we have r linear independent cointegration vectors given by the columns of $\boldsymbol{\gamma}$. If the rank is equal to n then every linear combination of the variables is stationary implying that the variables are stationary themselves. In the case of exactly one cointegration relation $\boldsymbol{\gamma}$ is a single cointegration vector. The term $\boldsymbol{\gamma}'\mathbf{z}_{t-1}$ is the equilibrium error, the deviation from the long-run equilibrium in the last period. If the rank is known, the parameters of the model can be estimated by maximum likelihood. This representation will be of importance in chapters 5 and 8, where short-run dynamics are analyzed. The relation between this representation and the triangular representation in the equations 2.5 and 2.6 is further examined in chapter 8. Since this approach is quite standard in the literature today I do not discuss the Johansen procedure further. A detailed exposition of the method can be found in Johansen (1995).

Before moving on to a discussion of modeling seasonality, some final remarks on the problem of testing for cointegration. The straightforward method, suggested by Engle and Granger (1987), is to use the standard ADF test on the residuals of an OLS estimation of the cointegration vector. If the variables are cointegrated, the test should reject the null hypothesis of a unit root in the residuals. Of course, the distribution of the test is different from the Dickey-Fuller distribution when applied to residuals of a cointegration regression. Response surfaces for this test have been estimated by MacKinnon (1994). Although this test has the advantage of being extremely simple, there are other tests that might be preferable, especially in terms of power (Haug, 1996). The trace test of Johansen (1988) amounts to a test on the rank of the matrix $\boldsymbol{\Pi}$. Since his estimator is the maximum likelihood estimator of the system, the test is based on the likelihood ratio principle. Other tests that will be used have been suggested by Stock and Watson (1988) and Phillips and Ouliaris (1990). A description of the involved statistics and the intuition behind these tests can be found in the Haug paper.

2.2 Modeling Seasonality

This section discusses some basic concepts concerning the issue of seasonality in time series that are important for the empirical part of the book. For this purpose it is useful to start with a short overview of the different models suggested in the literature and the tests that are generally performed to discriminate between these models. As in the previous section the discussion is limited to the methods that are finally used in the book.

Today, seasonality in a time series is no longer seen as something that can easily be "adjusted" with some standard statistical procedure. Traditional adjustment methods like the Census X-11 method assume that the time series can be separated in a seasonal and a nonseasonal component. This, however, may not be possible.[2] In light of this problem and because of other drawbacks (Ghysels and Perron, 1993) it is seen as preferable to specify a seasonal univariate model for each of the series under consideration and base the multivariate analysis on this. Because seasonality can be modeled in quite different ways, which can have important consequences for inference in the multivariate model, it is necessary to test possible specifications against each other. This section discusses the methods that will be extensively used in the empirical part. For this purpose the following notation is used. It is assumed that we have $n = 4 * N$ observations of some quarterly time series x_t. The sample can then be divided in four series X_{sT} with $s = 1, 2, 3, 4$ of length N, each containing the observations in quarter s for all years T.

[2] For an exposition of the arguments, see the survey by Franses (1996).

The commonly used seasonal models are of the three different types

1. deterministic models
2. stationary stochastic models
3. nonstationary stochastic models

or combinations of those. All models can be seen as an extension of the standard autoregressive moving average (ARMA) model:

$$\phi(L)x_t = a + \theta(L)\epsilon_t \ , \tag{2.30}$$

where $\phi(L)$ and $\theta(L)$ are polynomials in the lag operator L with all roots inside the unit circle, a is the intercept, and ϵ_t is white noise.

The first class models seasonality with deterministic dummy variables, which allow the intercept to differ between the seasons:

$$\phi(L)x_t = a + \mathbf{D}_t\boldsymbol{\alpha} + \theta(L)\epsilon_t \ , \tag{2.31}$$

where $\mathbf{D}_t$ is a matrix of seasonal dummies and $\boldsymbol{\alpha}$ are parameters. The seasonal pattern is therefore assumed to be constant over time.

Stationary seasonality is modeled by an ARMA model with seasonal autoregressive or moving average polynomials called SARMA model:

$$\phi_s(L)x_t = a + \theta_s(L)\epsilon_t \ , \tag{2.32}$$

where $\phi_s(L)$ and $\theta_s(L)$ take the form

$$\phi_s(L) = 1 - \phi_1 L^4 - \phi_2 L^8 - \cdots - \phi_p L^{4p} \tag{2.33}$$

$$\theta_s(L) = 1 + \theta_1 L^4 + \theta_2 L^8 + \cdots + \theta_q L^{4q} \ . \tag{2.34}$$

In the multiplicative SARMA model additional nonseasonal autoregressive and moving average polynomials are considered.

If the seasonality is assumed to be nonstationary this is reflected by seasonal unit roots in the autoregressive polynomial:

$$(1 + L)(1 + L^2)\phi(L)x_t = a + \theta(L)\epsilon_t \ . \tag{2.35}$$

A more detailed description of this model is given below. In all models it is possible to add a deterministic or stochastic trend component.

A first assessment on the nature of the seasonality can be made with a visual test. For this purpose one first removes the trend from the series by an appropriate detrending procedure and then plots the X_{sT} series in a diagram. This is called a skip sample plot and is used in chapter 7. If the seasonality is stationary or deterministic or both, the quarters should not display any trending behaviour. A further test, proposed by Franses (1996), would be to make recursive estimates of the dummy variable model and to plot the parameter estimates. This, however, can only deliver a first impression and should be followed by a statistical testing procedure.

A natural starting point for this is the approach of Hylleberg et al. (1990), called HEGY test, which extends the ADF test to the seasonal case. The null hypothesis is an autoregressive process of the form:

$$\phi(L)x_t = \epsilon_t \; . \tag{2.36}$$

They show that it is possible to factorize the polynomial $\phi(L)$ in the following way:

$$\begin{aligned}\phi(L) = & -\pi_1 L(1+L+L^2+L^3) - \pi_2(-L)(1-L+L^2-L^3) \\ & -(\pi_4+\pi_3 L)(-L)(1-L^2) + \phi^*(L)(1-L^4) \; ,\end{aligned} \tag{2.37}$$

where the π_i depend on the parameters of the polynomial. If the polynomial has unit roots at one of the seasonal frequencies or at the nonseasonal frequency, this corresponds to one of the π_i's being zero. The unit roots are given by the following factors:

$$(1-L)(1+L)(1-iL)(1+iL) = (1-L^4) \; , \tag{2.38}$$

which corresponds to a unit root at the zero frequency, the frequency π and the complex unit roots together at the frequency $\pi/2$. These frequencies imply no cycle, two cycles and one cycle per year. The test consists of simple t- and F-tests on the OLS estimates of the π_i's. The estimated equation is

$$\phi^*(L)y_{4t} = \pi_1 y_{1t-1} + \pi_2 y_{2t-1} + \pi_3 y_{3t-2} + \pi_4 y_{3t-1} + \epsilon_t \; , \tag{2.39}$$

where

$$y_{1t} = (1+L+L^2+L^3)x_t \tag{2.40}$$
$$y_{2t} = -(1-L+L^2-L^3)x_t \tag{2.41}$$
$$y_{3t} = -(1-L^2)x_t \tag{2.42}$$
$$y_{4t} = (1-L^4)x_t \; . \tag{2.43}$$

The test for the unit root at frequency zero is a t-test on π_1 with $\pi_1 < 0$ as the alternative. The same test applies for the unit root at the semiannual periodicity, which is a t-test on π_2 vs $\pi_2 < 0$. For the unit root at the annual periodicity, Hylleberg et al. propose using either an F-test on the joint significance of π_3 and π_4 or, alternatively, first test with a two-sided t-test the significance of π_4 and then in a one-sided test the significance of π_3 against $\pi_3 < 0$. This book uses the F-test.

Generally, the equation is augmented by a deterministic trend and seasonal dummies to give power to the alternative. As recent studies have shown, the right number of lagged fourth differences is of great importance for the performance of the test. In all applications of the test, the lag selection procedure suggested by Ghysels et al. (1993) is therefore used.

A second test was developed by Canova and Hansen (1995). They take the opposite route and start from a deterministic model. The idea behind the

CH-test is that if unit roots are present, these must show up in the estimated residual of the deterministic model. Their test can therefore be seen as the seasonal analogue to the unit root test of Kwiatkowski et al. (1992).

The null hypothesis is the following model for the detrended series:

$$x_t = a + \mathbf{z}_t'\beta + \mathbf{D}_t\boldsymbol{\alpha}_t + \epsilon_t \ , \tag{2.44}$$

which is a deterministic dummy variable model with a vector of exogenous variables $\mathbf{z}_t$ as additional regressors. The error process in this representation is allowed to be autocorrelated. For a univariate analysis Canova and Hansen suggest including one lag of the endogenous variable. This, however, can severely affect the power of the test if a unit root at frequency π is present, as shown by Hylleberg (1995), and should not be done.

Because I want to use the test complementary with the HEGY test, as is suggested by the Monte Carlo results of Hylleberg (1995), I restrict the exposition to the case of trigonometric dummies, which allow a direct interpretation of seasonality as cyclical. The dummies are given by

$$D_{t1} = cos(0.5\pi t) \tag{2.45}$$
$$D_{t2} = sin(0.5\pi t) \tag{2.46}$$
$$D_{t3} = cos(\pi t) \ , \tag{2.47}$$

where the first two dummies reflect an annual cycle and the last dummy a semiannual cycle. The model is a reparameterization of the standard dummy variable model and therefore leads to the same OLS-residuals $\hat{\epsilon}_t$.

The alternative is a unit root process for some or all of the parameters of the dummies given by

$$\mathbf{A}'\boldsymbol{\alpha}_t = \mathbf{A}'\boldsymbol{\alpha}_{t-1} + \mathbf{u}_t \ , \tag{2.48}$$

where $\mathbf{u}_t$ is a martingale difference sequence with full rank covariance matrix $\tau^2\mathbf{G}$. The matrix $\mathbf{A}$ is a selection matrix for the parameters depending on which unit roots are tested. Three possibilities are considered:

$$\mathbf{A}_1 = \mathbf{I}_3 \tag{2.49}$$
$$\mathbf{A}_2 = (\mathbf{I}_2 \quad \mathbf{0})' \tag{2.50}$$
$$\mathbf{A}_3 = (0 \quad 0 \quad 1)' \ . \tag{2.51}$$

This leads to three tests, a joint test for $\mathbf{A} = \mathbf{A}_1$, a test for a unit root at frequency $\pi/2$ for $\mathbf{A} = \mathbf{A}_2$ and a test for a unit root at frequency π for $\mathbf{A} = \mathbf{A}_3$.

The test is a Lagrange multiplier test with the null hypothesis of $H_0 : \tau = 0$ vs $H_1 : \tau > 0$. The test statistic is:

$$LM = \frac{1}{T^2}\,\text{trace}\left((\mathbf{A}'\hat{\boldsymbol{\Sigma}}\mathbf{A})^{-1}\sum_{i=1}^{T}\hat{\mathbf{F}}_i\hat{\mathbf{F}}_i'\mathbf{A}\right) \ , \tag{2.52}$$

with

$$\hat{\mathbf{F}}_i = \sum_{t=1}^{i} \mathbf{D}_t' \hat{\epsilon}_t \,, \tag{2.53}$$

where $\hat{\boldsymbol{\Sigma}}$ is an estimate of the long-run covariance matrix of the stationary process $\mathbf{D}_t'\epsilon_t$. A possible candidate is again the kernel estimator suggested by Newey and West (1987):

$$\hat{\boldsymbol{\Sigma}} = \sum_{k=-m}^{m} w\left(\frac{k}{m}\right) \frac{1}{n} \sum_t \mathbf{D}_{t+k}' \hat{\epsilon}_{t+k} \mathbf{D}_t \hat{\epsilon}_t \,, \tag{2.54}$$

where $w(.)$ is any kernel that produces positive semidefinite covariance estimates. I use a Bartlett kernel together with the bandwidth selection suggested by Andrews (1991). For large values of L the null hypothesis of deterministic seasonality is rejected in favor of a unit root at the given frequency. The distribution of the statistic is a generalized von Mises distribution VM(p) with p degrees of freedom. Canova and Hansen develop the following results:

$$LM_j \xrightarrow{d} VM(3) \tag{2.55}$$

$$LM_{\pi/2} \xrightarrow{d} VM(2) \tag{2.56}$$

$$LM_{\pi} \xrightarrow{d} VM(1) \,, \tag{2.57}$$

for a joint test, a test for a unit root at frequency $\pi/2$, and a test for a unit root at frequency π respectively. The distribution is tabulated in Canova and Hansen (1995)Canova and Hansen (1995).

Following Hylleberg (1995) I calculate both tests for every series, because the performance of the tests with respect to size and power differs, depending on the data generating process (DGP). If the tests deliver conflicting results, further examination is necessary. If, finally, a model is chosen for a particular series, it is possible to remove the seasonal unit roots with an appropriate seasonal filter. If the tests indicate a unit root at frequency π, the filter is $0.5(1 + L)$, and if they indicate a unit root at frequency $\pi/2$, the filter is $0.5(1 + L^2)$. In the case where both unit roots are present, this leads to the filter $0.25(1 + L + L^2 + L^3)$. The filtered series can then be used in the cointegration analysis. Stationary seasonality can be neglected, as the error process in the cointegration model is allowed to be serially correlated.

These basic ideas of modeling seasonality are easily extended to a multivariate framework, where an additional property has to be considered: the possibility of seasonal cointegration discussed in Hylleberg et al. (1990), Engle et al. (1993) and Lee (1992). If a number of series have a seasonal unit root, then a linear combination of these series may have only stationary seasonality. An intuition for this concept is that the change in the seasonal patterns of the series is caused by a common trending factor. An example would be global warming leading to a similar change of the seasonal patterns of output, employment etc. because of a less pronounced annual drop in construction in winter. For some sets of variables such a common trend in the seasonal pattern may be reasonable. In the main empirical part in chapter 7 of the book, the focus is on cointegration at the zero frequency, which is the standard form of cointegration introduced by Engle and Granger (1987). Things are different in chapter 5, however, where the dynamic interaction between actual and contract wages is analyzed and in chapter 8 where the dynamic interaction between the variables in the model for the natural rate plays a role. Here, it is important to consider the possibility of seasonal cointegration when using the seasonal ECM framework of Lee (1992) to avoid a misspecification of the model. A more detailed description of the model is given in chapter 5.

This ends the discussion of the most important concepts, estimators and tests that are used at several places in the book. The next chapter gives an overview of developments in the theoretical field of union-firm bargaining that forms the basis of the subsequent analysis.

3. The Union-Firm Bargain

In the beginning of research on wage determination under trade unionism it was not the form of the model that was contentious; the question was if it is feasible to assume a utility maximizing trade union at all. The different positions are well documented in two monographs by Arthur M. Ross and John T. Dunlop. Ross (1948) was very critical of attempts to model union behaviour in the standard way: "Among all the participants in economic life, the trade union is probably least suited to purely economic analysis" (p. 7). He was not against economic analysis in general, but he thought that the trade union is a political institution and the wage bargain is primarily influenced by nonquantifiable pressures, which cannot easily be incorporated in a formal model. In his opinion, a model that reduces the union to a kind of enterprise maximizing a simple objective function would be an undue abstraction that "so oversimplifies human behaviour as to leave it unrecognizable and unexplained" (p. 21). This view was challenged by Dunlop (1950). In the preface to the second edition of his book he states that "it is not to be denied that the institutions of the collective bargaining process have some independent effect on wage rates ... But the thesis must be rejected that wage determination under collective bargaining is to be explained most fundamentally or fruitfully in terms of a political process" (p. iii). When examining the future course of the economics of the trade union, one can only conclude that the view of Dunlop has succeeded in the long run. But one should keep in mind that the explanations and models discussed here are incomplete and the level of abstraction is clearly very high. Taken together with the data and aggregation problems one generally faces in empirical analysis, we should not be too optimistic regarding an empirically successful model of wage setting on the macroeconomic level. However, this should not hinder attempts to model union behaviour as primarily economic in nature and base statistical models of wage setting on such an analysis. In the end, for an economist, this is the natural route to follow.

The economic theory of the trade union was long dominated by the model of a monopoly union which acts like a seller of labour, facing either a downward sloping demand curve for labour as in Dunlop (1950), or facing a monopsonistic firm leading to a bilateral monopoly as suggested by Fellner (1947). On the side of the firm, the discussion concentrated on the degree of market power in both factor and product markets. Dunlop gives an extensive discussion of the implications of different possible constellations. Most important, of course, is the position of the firm in the labour market, leading to the two mentioned cases. On the side of the union, the specification of the utility has been contentious. Dunlop makes several proposals, e.g. wage bill maximization. This topic is still unresolved and will be discussed later.

A major problem of the bilateral monopoly model has been indeterminacy. Generally, it is only possible to specify a range of outcomes that seem plausible, because they are Pareto efficient and individually rational, as discussed in Leontief (1946). This is the contract curve. Which point on the contract curve is realized, however, is not predicted by the model. This unsatisfactory state of the theory was resolved by the advent of formal bargaining theory in the early fifties. Until the contributions of Nash (1950, 1953) the only available formal bargaining model was that of Zeuthen (1930). Surprisingly, the model found little response in the literature until the fifties, as noted by Pen (1959). Pen seems to be the first labour economist who fully appreciated the contribution of Zeuthen in the 1950 Dutch edition of his monograph. The publication of Nash's work stimulated interest in bargaining theory and lead to an important paper by Harsanyi (1956), who shows that both models lead to the same bargaining solution and are therefore formally equivalent. The approach is quite different, however. The Zeuthen model explicitly models a dynamic bargaining process in which the parties make alternating concessions, leading to an equilibrium. The axiomatic approach of Nash, in contrast, is static in nature and defines a solution in terms of mathematical properties that are assumed to be sensible in the given context. Because of the formal equivalence, the Nash-Zeuthen model, as it is called by Harsanyi, can be applied irrespective of what approach is preferred. It was therefore readily adopted by trade union theorists[1] and stands at the center of modern trade union theory. This did not lead to a total abandonment of the monopoly union model, which has been a quite popular model for a long time[2] and is still alive in the discussion in more or less unchanged form. But the focus of research shifted towards the specific features of the bargaining model.

At the center of the discussion are two models: the efficient-bargaining model, discussed in de Menil (1971) and McDonald and Solow (1981), and the right-to-manage model by Nickell and Andrews (1983). The efficient-bargaining model is essentially the bilateral monopoly model, where the point on the contract curve is determined by the bargaining solution. To reach this point, the union and the firm generally have to bargain over both wages and employment. It is possible that the firm is not on its labour demand curve. In the right-to-manage model the union and the firm bargain only over the wage,

[1] A theoretical and empirical analysis of the Nash-Zeuthen model is made e.g. in de Menil (1971).

[2] The monograph by Cartter (1959) still focuses mainly on the monopoly model.

and the firm is on its labour demand curve, as in the monopoly union model of Dunlop (1950) These models are therefore often named *labour demand models*. Since the beginning of the eighties a large literature has evolved where these models have been critically discussed and empirically tested.

Since the monopoly union model is quite simple and not a bargaining model, a short formal exposition is given here. In this model it is assumed that the union has the power to set wages, while the firm has the power to set employment. Its labour demand curve is given by

$$L = L(w, \mathbf{q}) , \tag{3.1}$$

where w is the nominal wage, and $\mathbf{q}$ is a vector of other factors influencing labour demand. The union simply maximizes its utility

$$U = U(w, L(w, \mathbf{q}), \mathbf{m}) , \tag{3.2}$$

depending on the wage, the labour demand and a vector of other factors $\mathbf{m}$. The monopoly union wage therefore is given by:

$$w^* = \underset{w}{\operatorname{argmax}} U(w, L(w, \mathbf{q}), \mathbf{m}) . \tag{3.3}$$

As discussed in Fedeli (1994), the comparative statics of this model are not determined with general forms of the utility and the labour demand function. It is necessary to put more structure on the model, i.e. to assume specific functional forms, to get clear results. The details of the argument are not discussed here, since this property is dealt with later in the context of the right-to-manage model. The next section gives a short, formal description of the bargaining models.

3.1 Bargaining Models

The discussion here serves the purpose of a short introduction. For surveys of the literature on union-firm bargaining models see Oswald (1985), Holmlund (1989), Booth (1995) and Manzini (1998). In the right-to-manage model the union bargains with the firm only about the wage. Union utility has the same form as in the monopoly union model. The utility of the firm is generally assumed to be given by (real) pure economic profits

$$\pi = \pi(w, \mathbf{q}) \tag{3.4}$$

that depend on the same variables as the labour demand function[3].

A bargaining problem exists, because the union utility increases in the wage, while firm profits decrease in the wage, at least for a certain range

[3] Of course, the vector $\mathbf{q}$ might include variables that do not affect labour demand.

of wages. In bargaining theory it is assumed that both parties have a disagreement or fallback point, i.e. the value of their utilities when no bargain is reached. Of course, no party would accept a bargaining outcome that gives it less than this fallback utility. In the following discussion, utilities are generally stated as net utilities with a disagreement point of zero, either because the fallback utility has been subtracted from an assumed gross utility, or because the disagreement point is zero by assumption. These net utilities are zero for a certain wage called the reservation wage. The reservation wage of the firm $\bar{r}$ is given by

$$\pi(\bar{r}, \mathbf{q}) = 0 . \tag{3.5}$$

The reservation wage of the union r^* is defined as

$$U(r^*, L(r^*, \mathbf{q}), \mathbf{m}) = 0 . \tag{3.6}$$

The bargaining problem can be visualized in a diagram by plotting all possible combinations of profits and union utility for different wages. This is done in figure 3.1. The line of possible utility combinations has a negative slope for all wages that are smaller than the monopoly union wage. The utilities of both bargaining parties for the monopoly union wage are indicated by ϕ^{mu}. The line intersects the vertical and horizontal axis at the reservation wages. The central question in bargaining theory is: Which point on the line is chosen by the bargaining parties? This is the problem of the bargaining solution that plays an important role in this book. A more detailed and formal discussion of this topic is deferred to the next chapter. For the exposition here, a short introduction of the most widely used solution should be sufficient.

In the empirical and theoretical literature on union-firm bargaining the generalized Nash bargaining solution is applied almost exclusively. It can be calculated by maximizing the following weighted product with weights $(1-\chi, \chi)$:

$$\Omega = (\pi)^{1-\chi}(U)^{\chi} \qquad \chi \in [0, 1] . \tag{3.7}$$

The bargained wage is therefore given by

$$\tilde{w} = \operatorname*{argmax}_{w} \Omega . \tag{3.8}$$

The first order condition can be written as

$$\epsilon_{Uw} = \frac{1-\chi}{\chi} \epsilon_{\pi w} , \tag{3.9}$$

where $\epsilon_{Uw}, \epsilon_{\pi w}$ denote the (positive) elasticities of U, π with respect to w. If U is multiplicatively separable in L and can be written as

$$U = u(w, \mathbf{m}) L(w, \mathbf{q})^{\beta} , \tag{3.10}$$

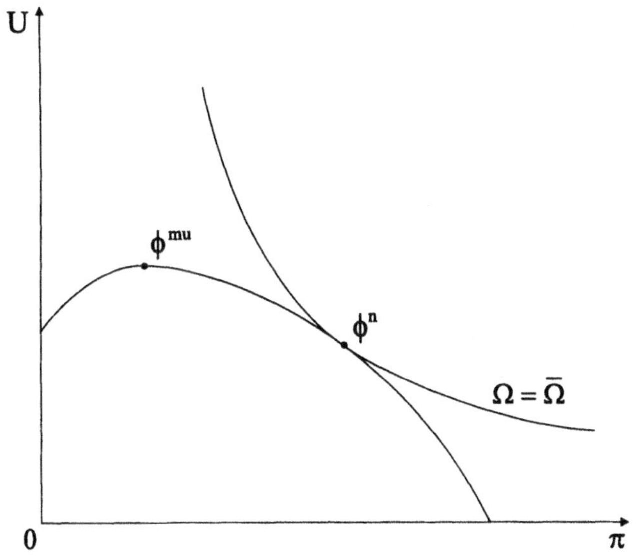

Fig. 3.1. The bargaining problem

where u is a subutility, the first order condition is

$$\epsilon_{uw} - \beta\epsilon_{Lw} = \frac{1-\chi}{\chi}\epsilon_{\pi w} \,. \tag{3.11}$$

This solution is indicated by ϕ^n in figure 3.1. At this point the value of the hyperbole defined for some fixed $\Omega = \bar{\Omega}$ is maximized.

It is clear that the bargained wage will be in the interval (w^*, r^*), because

$$\lim_{\chi \to 1} \tilde{w} = w^* \tag{3.12}$$

and the union does not accept any wage below r^*. The solution can also be displayed in a $w - L$ diagram. The interval is shown in figure 3.2 as ϕ^{rtm}.

In the efficient bargaining model the union and the firm bargain over both wages and employment. Therefore, the firm does not optimize its labour input and profit is a function of wage and employment $\pi = \pi(w, L, \mathbf{q})$. For any given vectors $\mathbf{q}$ and $\mathbf{m}$ it is then possible to draw isoprofit curves (IP) for the firm and indifference curves (IC) for the union in the $w - L$ diagram as shown in figure 3.2. As can be seen, compared to the right-to-manage model, it is possible to raise the utility of one of the bargaining parties while holding the utility of the other party constant. Bargaining over wages *and* employment can therefore lead to a Pareto improvement. Using again the generalized Nash bargain, the solution is given by

$$(\tilde{w}, \tilde{L}) = \underset{w,L}{\operatorname{argmax}}\, \Omega \,, \tag{3.13}$$

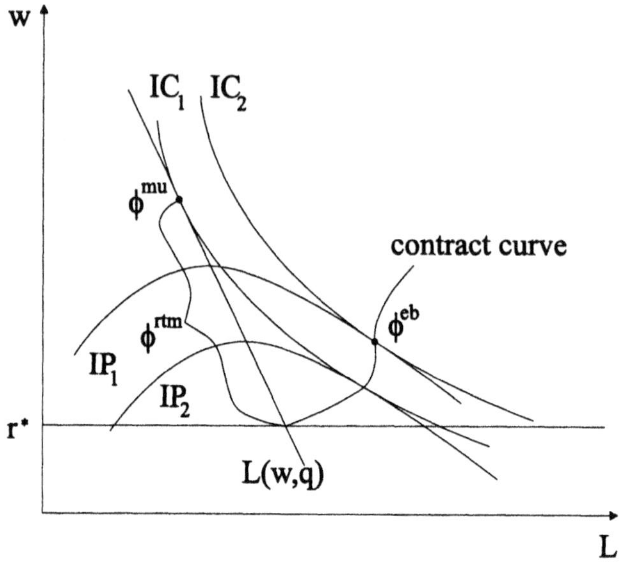

Fig. 3.2. Bargaining models

which implies two first order conditions

$$\epsilon_{Uw} = \frac{1-\chi}{\chi}\epsilon_{\pi w} \tag{3.14}$$

$$\epsilon_{UL} = \frac{1-\chi}{\chi}\epsilon_{\pi L}\ . \tag{3.15}$$

Dividing the first equation by the second leads to the following condition:

$$\frac{\frac{\partial U}{\partial w}}{\frac{\partial U}{\partial L}} = \frac{\frac{\partial \pi}{\partial w}}{\frac{\partial \pi}{\partial L}}\ . \tag{3.16}$$

Therefore, the solution implies that isoprofit and indifference curves are tangent. For different values of χ one gets the contract curve of all possible bargaining outcomes. The efficient bargaining solution ϕ^{eb} and the contract curve are also shown in figure 3.2.

Because the implications of these models can be quite different, it is of major interest which model should be applied. A major contribution has been the work of Alogoskoufis and Manning (1991), where an empirical discrimination between all three models is developed and carried out with British data. However, it seems that there are a lot of researchers who prefer one of the models on a priori reasons (see Nickell and Andrews, 1983, for Britain). Especially for Germany,[4] the question of the correct bargaining model is not

[4] For an overview of the institutional features of wage bargaining in Germany see Carruth and Schnabel (1993).

very contentious. Since the monopoly union model is an extreme, special case of the right-to-manage model and bargaining over employment, as in the efficient bargaining model, is not possible with an employers association representing hundreds or thousands of firms, the right-to-manage model is widely accepted. For this reason the next section and the rest of the book will concentrate on this model.

3.2 Empirical Tests

The first empirical implementation of the right-to-manage model was the paper by Nickell and Andrews (1983). The authors develop a pair of equations from the bargaining model where the first one is a wage equation and can be seen as a linear approximation of equation (3.9) for a given specification of union and firm utility. The second one is a standard labour demand function. These two equations also form the basis of a large part of the more recent studies. In the short survey in this section, I want to concentrate on the articles that use the tools of modern time series analysis with aggregate data as in this book.

There are several papers that fall into this category. For the U.K. there is a paper by Darby and Wren-Lewis (1993), there is a recent test for Belgium by Hecq and Mahy (1997) and two articles with Finnish data by Tyrväinen (1995b, 1992). For Germany there is a cointegration study for the wage equation by Carruth and Schnabel (1993) and a broader international analysis, including Germany, has been done in Tyrväinen (1995a). The modest purpose here is to highlight some features of these studies that seem to be of special importance for the approach in this book.

An important factor in the evaluation of empirical studies of the bargaining model is the problem of identification. The identification of a (structural) wage equation based on equation (3.9) is questioned by Manning (1993). Because of Hotelling's lemma, the elasticity of profit with respect to the wage can be written as labour demand times the wage divided by profit:

$$\epsilon_{\pi w} = L \frac{w}{\pi} \, . \tag{3.17}$$

If profit is substituted by its determinants $\mathbf{q}$, a loglinear approximation might therefore include labour demand as well as all variables determining profit. These variables generally also affect labour demand. If union utility includes labour demand, then ϵ_{Uw} generally depends on $\mathbf{q}$ as well, and this delivers a further reason to include them in a wage equation. However, if the wage equation includes labour demand as an independent variable as well as all variables affecting labour demand, then the equation is clearly not identified, because none of the variables in the labour demand equation is excluded from the wage equation. A related identification problem is raised when the wage equation includes average labour productivity on the right hand side.[5] Under perfect competition the first order condition of a profit minimizing firm with Cobb-Douglas technology implies that average productivity is simply a multiple of real wages. Therefore Manning (1995a) concludes: "It is remarkable that so many economists find it interesting that the wage is correlated with the average product of labour and think that this tells us anything about the operation of labour markets" (p. 260).

Unfortunately, both studies of the German labour market mentioned above are affected by this critique. In the study by Carruth and Schnabel (1993), the long-run relation takes the form:

$$\ln W_t = \beta_0 + \beta_1 \ln P_{ct} + \beta_2 \ln Q_t + \beta_3 U_t + \epsilon_t \ , \tag{3.18}$$

where W_t is nominal contract wages, P_{ct} is the consumer price index, Q_t is average labour productivity and U_t is the unemployment rate. The estimated coefficients are $\hat{\beta}_1 = 1.09, \hat{\beta}_2 = 0.95, \hat{\beta}_3 = -1.86$. Therefore, the logs of real wages and average productivity are approximately related with a unit coefficient. Except for the significance of the unemployment rate, this is exactly the result one would expect from a first order condition for labour demand. This makes an interpretation quite difficult. The tax wedge, defined here as the ratio of real labour costs to the firm and the net real consumption wage of the employees, was not significant. From this result Carruth and Schnabel conclude that: "In the long-run ... rises in the wedge seem to be entirely borne by labour" (p. 307). This contrasts with the findings of another article using German data.

In the study of Tyrväinen (1995a) the estimated wage equation for Germany is quite similar. The real producer wage is related to average productivity and a set of other variables. The Johansen procedure used in this article detects four cointegration vectors for the included variables. The wage equation is identified in the cointegration space by a parameter restriction leading to the following preferred specification:

$$\ln \frac{W_{at}}{P_t} = \ln \frac{P_{ct}}{P_t} + \ln Q_t - 0.17\, U_t + \ln(1 - T_t) + \epsilon_t \ , \tag{3.19}$$

where W_{at} is the average wage, P_t is a value-added deflator and T_t is the average income tax. Although the tax variable is different, the result concerning taxes is more or less the opposite of the result in Carruth and Schnabel (1993). Tyrväinen finds strong real wage resistance in Germany. All tax increases are shifted on the employers in the long-run. In a second estimation it is verified that the logs of average productivity and real labour costs $\ln(W_{at}(1+S_t)/P_t)$, where S_t are social insurance contributions of the employers, are cointegrated with a unit coefficient. The difference between the equations is mainly the chosen wage and price variables and the inclusion of taxes and unemployment

[5] A theoretical argument for this practice in the framework of the right-to-manage model can be found in Darby and Wren-Lewis (1993).

in the wage equation. Whether this tells us something about wage setting or about the relation between prices, taxes, social insurance contributions and unemployment is debatable. The same holds for the Tyrväinen (1995b) paper with Finnish data. Again, average productivity is included in the wage equation.

These identification problems in the wage equation are quite severe and not easily overcome. The approach in this book will be to estimate a reduced form employment equation where these identification problems do not arise as will be shown later. This is similar to the approach in Tyrväinen (1992) for Finland. Employment is not included in the wage equation. However, in this study the reduced employment equation contains productivity variables like the capital stock. As discussed later, this is not very convincing, because it does not conform to a view of the labour market where in the long-run productivity changes are neutral towards employment. In the study of Hecq and Mahy (1997) identification is achieved by excluding average productivity from the wage equation. As a justification for this they refer to Manning (1993). Manning argues that structural wage equations should not include productivity terms. However, his reasoning does not suggest that wages do not depend on productivity. On the contrary, wages fully adjust to productivity changes in his model. His structural static equation describing wage setting does not explicitly include wages at all and simply relates unemployment to a set of other variables: the replacement ratio, union density, tax progressivity and the output-capital ratio. In this respect the model is quite similar to the reduced form employment equation that is derived later. What is true is that the wage bargaining model often leads to wage equations that do not include productivity variables. This, however, makes it unreasonable as a model of long-run wage determination. The issue is further discussed in the next chapter.

An interesting study is the cointegration analysis is Darby and Wren-Lewis (1993). They develop a wage equation with average productivity and a set of other variables on the right hand side like the other studies mentioned above. They conduct unit root tests for all variables in their model and conclude that these variables contain a stochastic trend. As suggested by the argument made above, they find a cointegration relation for real wages and average productivity in the UK. The test of the bargaining model in their paper rests on the argument that even when the wage equation is not identified a necessary condition for the model to be valid is the existence of a second cointegration relation for the other variables in the wage equation, given by unemployment, unionisation and unemployment benefits in their model. The evidence for such a relation is weak, however, for the UK and they argue: "The fact that an economically plausible linear combination of these variables should fail to account for the rise in unemployment in the 1980s is not surprising, as both benefits and unionisation declined over this period." This is in line with the arguments of Manning (1995a) that standard bargaining models are not capable of explaining the recent rise in unemployment and, as should be clear from the introduction, it is argued in this book that one of the possible reasons for this is a neglected variable, namely the capital income tax. Why this variable is is not considered in most studies is explained in the next chapter.

4. The Bargaining Solution

The dominance of the generalized Nash bargaining solution (GNBS) in the wage bargaining literature could be due to the fact that it is widely used and can be rationalized by a strategic game (Binmore et al., 1986). However, there are several reasons why another solution concept may be preferable. In axiomatic bargaining game theory the appropriateness of a solution concept hinges crucially on its axiomatic characterization. As will be argued, the axioms of the proportional solution (PS), introduced by Kalai (1977), are more reasonable than the axioms of the GNBS in the union-firm context, because they conform to a notion of fairness that is often emphasized in wage negotiations by the bargaining parties. Experimental studies support the relevance of this issue. An implication of this difference is that a proportional tax on the utility of the firm that does not influence the bargained wage under the GNBS is of importance for wage negotiations under the PS. Moreover, application of the PS to this problem is interesting for the following reasons.

First, the Nash solution is defined only for compact convex bargaining sets[1] (Nash, 1950). In the right-to-manage model this condition is not always fulfilled, as Alexander and Ledermann (1994, 1996) show. An example is given below. Second, the comparative statics of the GNBS depend on the specific form of the assumed utility functions. It is not sufficient to specify whether a variable increases or decreases utility to get stable results. Therefore, the right-to-manage model suffers from the same lack of empirical content as the monopoly union model. This problem is mitigated when the PS is applied. Third, for standard utilities the comparative statics can be quite different when the PS is applied. The GNBS often leads to the result that productivity does not influence the bargained wage. Therefore, the model is seen as an explanation of the wage stickiness over the business cycle (McDonald and Solow, 1981). As is shown, the wage under the PS often depends on productivity. For special utilities, wages fully adapt to changes in productivity. This leads to an interpretation of the model as a description of the long-run behaviour of wages. These results suggest that the robustness of the bargaining model is not only called into question because of technological assumptions,

[1] Of course, there are other ways to overcome at least the convexity restriction (Conley and Wilkie, 1996).

as argued by Manning (1994), but also because the bargaining solution that is employed could be the wrong one.

After some important concepts have been defined in the next section, section 4.2 derives the allocation set in the right-to-manage model and discusses the significance of the possible nonconvexity. The PS is characterized and extended to noncompact, nonconvex allocation sets in section 4.3. In section 4.4 the reasons for the application of the PS to this problem are stated and section 4.5 discusses several possible caveats against this solution.

4.1 Definitions

In contrast to chapter 3 the material presented here is quite formal and uses the concepts of axiomatic bargaining game theory. To facilitate the discussion it is therefore useful to clarify some technical language. An N-person bargaining problem consists of a pair $(\mathbf{S}, \mathbf{d})$ where $\mathbf{S}$ is a nonempty subset of $\mathbb{R}^N$, and $\mathbf{d} \in \mathbf{S}$. The set $\mathbf{S}$, called allocation set or bargaining set, is the set of all possible utility allocations that are attainable through cooperation of all N individuals. If no agreement is reached, then the outcome of the game is $\mathbf{d}$, the disagreement or fallback point. A bargaining solution ϕ, defined on a class of problems Σ^N, is a mapping of each $(\mathbf{S}, \mathbf{d}) \in \Sigma^N$ to a point in $\mathbf{S}$.

The vector inequalities are given by $\leq, <, \ll$. A allocation set $\mathbf{S}$ is called $\mathbf{d}$-comprehensive if the following condition holds:

$$\mathbf{d} \leq \mathbf{x} \leq \mathbf{y} \wedge \mathbf{y} \in \mathbf{S} \Rightarrow \mathbf{x} \in \mathbf{S} .$$

This property ensures that both parties are able to dispose part of their utility. Every point that implies less or the same utility for both parties than some other point in the bargaining set has also to be in $\mathbf{S}$.

The comprehensive hull of a set $\mathbf{S} \subset \mathbb{R}^N$ with respect to a point $\mathbf{d} \in \mathbb{R}^N$ is the smallest $\mathbf{d}$-comprehensive set containing $\mathbf{S}$:

$$\text{com}(\mathbf{S}, \mathbf{d}) \equiv \{\mathbf{x} \in \mathbb{R}^N \mid \mathbf{x} \in \mathbf{S} \text{ or } \exists \mathbf{y} \in \mathbf{S} \text{ such that } \mathbf{d} \leq \mathbf{x} \leq \mathbf{y}\} . \tag{4.1}$$

This is a simple way to fill holes in a given bargaining set that would violate the assumption of free disposal.

The convex hull of a set $\mathbf{S} \subset \mathbb{R}^N$ is the smallest convex set containing $\mathbf{S}$:

$$\text{con}(\mathbf{S}) \equiv \{\mathbf{x} \in \mathbb{R}^N \mid \mathbf{x} = \sum_{i=1}^{N} \lambda_i \mathbf{y}_i, \sum_{i=1}^{N} \lambda_i = 1, \lambda_i \geq 0 \forall i, \text{and}\, \mathbf{y}_i \in \mathbf{S} \forall i\} . \tag{4.2}$$

This is another way of filling holes. It does not imply free disposal. On the other hand, it is stricter than comprehensiveness, because it does not permit any indentation. The combination of both concepts leads to $\text{comv}(\mathbf{S}, \mathbf{d}) := \text{com}(\text{con}(\mathbf{S}), \mathbf{d})$, the smallest $\mathbf{d}$-comprehensive convex set containing $\mathbf{S}$.

The next two definitions should be standard. For $\mathbf{S} \subset \mathbb{R}^N$, let

$$W(\mathbf{S}) := \{\mathbf{x} \in \mathbf{S} \mid \nexists \mathbf{y} \in \mathbf{S} \text{ with } \mathbf{y} \gg \mathbf{x}\} \tag{4.3}$$

denote the weakly Pareto optimal subset of **S** and

$$P(\mathbf{S}) := \{\mathbf{x} \in \mathbf{S} \mid \nexists \mathbf{y} \in \mathbf{S} \text{ with } \mathbf{y} > \mathbf{x}\} \tag{4.4}$$

the Pareto optimal subset of **S**.

4.2 The Allocation Set

As noted above, I consider only the right-to-manage model of bargaining here. A short discussion of the proportional solution in the framework of an efficient bargaining model can be found in McDonald and Solow (1981). In this model the possible allocations are given by all combinations of (π, U) for different wages $w > 0$. As before, the disagreement point $\mathbf{d}$ is assumed to be normalized to $(0,0)'$. This is innocuous because both solution concepts covary with additive transformations: $\phi(\mathbf{a}+\mathbf{S}, \mathbf{a}+\mathbf{d}) = \mathbf{a} + \phi(\mathbf{S}, \mathbf{d}) \, \forall \, \mathbf{a} \in \mathbb{R}^N$.

When the exogenous factors are taken as given, the profit and labour demand functions can be written as $\pi(w, \mathbf{q}) = g(w)$ and $L(w, \mathbf{q}) = l(w)$. The same holds for union utility $U(w, l(w), \mathbf{p}) = h(w)$. It is assumed that $g'(w) < 0$, $l'(w) < 0$ and $h'(w) > 0$. Assuming that $U \geq 0$ for $w \geq r^* \geq 0$ and $\pi \geq 0$ for $w \leq \bar{r} \leq \infty$, the individually rational and Pareto optimal allocations $\mathbf{A}$ are given for w in the range $r^* \leq w \leq \bar{r}$. The set $\mathbf{A}$ can be represented by a function $U = f(\pi)$ with $f' < 0$.

If one allows for free disposal of profits/utility, the set of possible allocations can be extended to the set $\bar{\mathbf{A}} = \text{com}(\mathbf{A}, \mathbf{0})$. The properties of $\bar{\mathbf{A}}$ are determined by the specific form of the assumed production and utility functions. The possibility of nonconvex allocation sets is discussed in Alexander and Ledermann (1996). It is straightforward that $\bar{\mathbf{A}}$ is convex if and only if $f'' \leq 0$. The inverse of g is denoted by g^{-1}. Then f can be written as $f = h(g^{-1}(\pi))$. The first derivative of f is then $f' = h' g^{-1'}$ and the second derivative is:

$$f'' = h'' g^{-1'} g^{-1'} + h' g^{-1''} \, . \tag{4.5}$$

We have $g^{-1'} < 0$ and $h' > 0$. For a wide range of profit and utility functions it is therefore possible that $f'' > 0$ and $\bar{\mathbf{A}}$ is not convex. Alexander and Ledermann derive sufficient conditions, e.g. on the utility and profit functions, leading to a convex bargaining set. However, the authors do not discuss whether the possible nonconvexity poses a problem in cases that are interesting from an economic perspective. An example can shed light on this question.

The Nash solution is illustrated in figure 4.1. As in figure 3.1 the solution point is found by shifting the hyperbole given for fixed $\Omega = \bar{\Omega}$ in equation (3.7) outwards to the frontier of the bargaining set. For the bargaining set with branch I such a point is given by ϕ^n. Assume now that the bargaining set changes to branch II. This affects the solution point in several possible ways. If there is a point of tangency of the hyperbole with the new branch below infinity, then this will be the new solution. If there is no such point the maximum attainable Ω is infinity, which under many union utilities implies a wage of infinity as well. It is questionable whether this is a reasonable result for this bargaining set. At certain critical points even a small change in the bargaining set can lead to a large change in the solution. The following example shows that these problems are not confined to perverse cases.

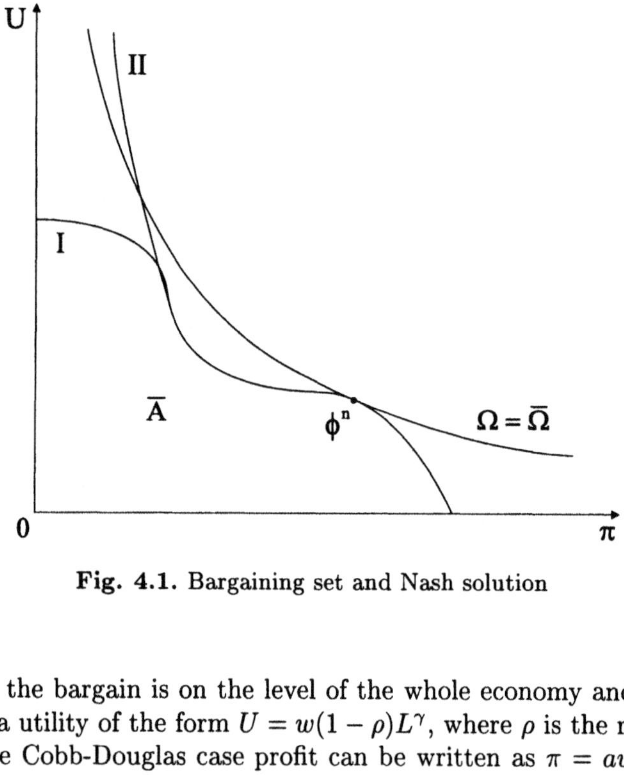

Fig. 4.1. Bargaining set and Nash solution

Assume the bargain is on the level of the whole economy and the union maximizes a utility of the form $U = w(1-\rho)L^{\gamma}$, where ρ is the replacement ratio. In the Cobb-Douglas case profit can be written as $\pi = aw^{-\delta}z$ where a and δ are constants and z is a function of other factor prices and the technology parameter. The corresponding labour demand function is $L = \delta aw^{-\delta-1}z$ and union utility is given by

$$U = w(1-\rho)(\delta aw^{-\delta-1}z)^{\gamma} . \tag{4.6}$$

To assure that union utility increases in the wage assume that $\gamma < \frac{1}{1+\delta}$.

The bargaining set is nonconvex and unbounded in this example, because the Pareto optimal set of the bargaining set can be written as:

$$U = \left(\frac{1}{az}\pi\right)^{-\frac{1-\gamma(\delta+1)}{\delta}} (1-\rho)(\delta a z)^{\gamma} = \kappa\pi^{-\epsilon},\ \epsilon > 0\,. \tag{4.7}$$

It might be argued that this is not very reasonable, because it implies that a monopoly union would set wages to infinity. However, it might nonetheless be a valid description of the bargaining set for a broad range of wages.

4.3 The Proportional Solution

A solution ϕ is called proportional if there exists a vector of weights $\mathbf{p} = (p_1, \ldots, p_N)' \gg \mathbf{0}$ with $\sum_{i \in N} p_i = 1$ such that for every $(\mathbf{S}, \mathbf{d})$, $\phi(\mathbf{S}, \mathbf{d}) = \mathbf{d} + \lambda(\mathbf{S}, \mathbf{d})\mathbf{p}$ where $\lambda(\mathbf{S}, \mathbf{d}) = \max\{t \mid \mathbf{d} + t\mathbf{p} \in \mathbf{S}\}$. A proportional solution with weight vector $\mathbf{p}$ is called $\phi^{\mathbf{p}}$. The condition $\mathbf{p} \gg \mathbf{0}$ is stronger than the usual condition $\mathbf{p} > \mathbf{0}$. This is necessary to allow for possible unbounded allocation sets.

As will be shown, this solution concept can be applied to bargaining games with noncompact, nonconvex allocation sets and is characterized by the following axioms:

1. Strong Monotonicity (SMON): For all $(\mathbf{S}, \mathbf{d}), (\mathbf{T}, \mathbf{d}) \in \Sigma^N$ with $\mathbf{S} \subset \mathbf{T}$, $\phi(\mathbf{T}, \mathbf{d}) \geq \phi(\mathbf{S}, \mathbf{d})$.
2. Weak Pareto Optimality (WPO): For every $(\mathbf{S}, \mathbf{d}) \in \Sigma^N$, $\phi(\mathbf{S}, \mathbf{d}) \in W(\mathbf{S})$.
3. Homogeneity (HOM): For every $(\mathbf{S}, \mathbf{d}) \in \Sigma^N$ and all $a > 0$ and $\mathbf{b} \in \mathbb{R}^N$, if $(a\mathbf{S} + \mathbf{b}, a\mathbf{d} + \mathbf{b}) \in \Sigma^N$, then $\phi(a\mathbf{S} + \mathbf{b}, a\mathbf{d} + \mathbf{b}) = a\phi(\mathbf{S}, \mathbf{d}) + \mathbf{b}$.
4. Strong Individual Rationality (SIR): For every $(\mathbf{S}, \mathbf{d}) \in \Sigma^N$, $\phi(\mathbf{S}, \mathbf{d}) \gg \mathbf{d}$ if and only if there exists a $\mathbf{x} \in \mathbf{S}$ with $\mathbf{x} \gg \mathbf{d}$.

The solution can be extended to the class of games H^N with closed, $\mathbf{d}$-comprehensive $\mathbf{S}$, $\mathbf{S} \subset \mathbb{R}^N$ and $\exists \mathbf{b} \in \mathbb{R}^N, \mathbf{b} \in \mathbf{S}, \mathbf{b} \gg \mathbf{d}$ with $\mathbf{S} \subset \mathbb{R}^N \setminus \{\mathbf{x} \mid \mathbf{x} \in \mathbb{R}^N, \mathbf{x} \gg \mathbf{b}\}$. The assumption about the existence of a point $\mathbf{b}$ with certain characteristics is necessary to exclude allocation sets that comprise all points larger than $\mathbf{d}$, which are of no practical importance. A graphical representation is given in figure 4.2.

Proposition 4.1
For every $\mathbf{p} \gg \mathbf{0}$ with $\sum_{i \in N} p_i = 1$ and for every $(\mathbf{S}, \mathbf{d}) \in H^N$ there exists exactly one $\phi^{\mathbf{p}}$.

Proof: From $\exists \mathbf{b}, \mathbf{b} \gg \mathbf{d}$ it follows that $\exists \mathbf{y}_l, \mathbf{d} \ll \mathbf{y}_l \ll \mathbf{b}, \mathbf{y}_l = t\mathbf{p} + \mathbf{d}$ for some $t > 0$. Because $\mathbf{S}$ is $\mathbf{d}$-comprehensive and $\mathbf{b} \in \mathbf{S}$ it follows that $\mathbf{y}_l \in \mathbf{S}$. Because $\mathbf{S} \subset \mathbb{R}^N \setminus \{\mathbf{x} \mid \mathbf{x} \in \mathbb{R}^N, \mathbf{x} \gg \mathbf{b}\}, \exists \mathbf{y}_u, \mathbf{y}_u = t\mathbf{p} + \mathbf{d}$ for some $t > 0$ with

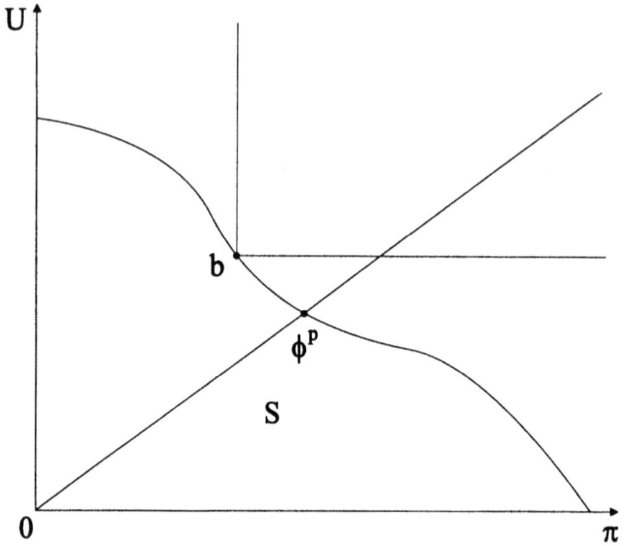

Fig. 4.2. Allocation set and PS

$\mathbf{y}_u \gg \mathbf{b} \Rightarrow \mathbf{y}_u \ni \mathbf{S}$. Since $\mathbf{S}$ is closed and $\mathbf{d}$-comprehensive and the real line is connected there exists exactly one $\mathbf{y}_m$ with $\mathbf{y}_l \ll \mathbf{y}_m \ll \mathbf{y}_u, \mathbf{y}_m \in \mathbf{S}, \mathbf{y}_m = t\mathbf{p} + \mathbf{d}$ for some $t > 0$ and $\{\mathbf{y} \mid \mathbf{y} \gg \mathbf{y}_m \wedge \mathbf{y} \in \mathbf{S}\} = \emptyset$. ■

The following theorem is a simple extension to theorem 4.30 in Peters (1992), p. 76f. to the extended allocation set.

Theorem 4.1
Let $\phi : H^N \to \mathbb{R}^N$ be a bargaining solution. Then ϕ satisfies HOM, SMON, WPO, and SIR if and only if it is proportional.

The proof of theorem 4.30 in Peters (1992) goes through for this case with minimal changes. Because of HOM it is sufficient to analyze a game with $\mathbf{d}$ normalize to zero.

Proof: Clearly $\phi^{\mathbf{P}}$ satisfies the four axioms. Assume ϕ satisfies HOM, SMON, WPO, and SIR. Let $\mathbf{e}^i, i \in N$ be the vector in $\mathbb{R}^N$ with a one in position i and zeros elsewhere. Let $\boldsymbol{\Delta}^N = \text{comv}\left(\{\mathbf{e}^i \in \mathbb{R}^N, i \in N\}, \mathbf{0}\right)$ and $\mathbf{p} := \phi(\boldsymbol{\Delta}^N)$. The proof will be completed by proving the following three statements:

1. $\phi(\mathbf{S}) \geq \phi^{\mathbf{P}}(\mathbf{S})$
2. If $\phi^{\mathbf{P}}(\mathbf{S}) \in P(\mathbf{S})$ then $\phi(\mathbf{S}) = \phi^{\mathbf{P}}(\mathbf{S})$
3. $\phi(\mathbf{S}) \leq \phi^{\mathbf{P}}(\mathbf{S})$

Because of SIR $\mathbf{p} \gg \mathbf{0}$. For $\epsilon > 0$ with $\epsilon < \min\{1 - p_i : i \in N\}$, define

$$\mathbf{V}^\epsilon = \text{comv}\left(\{\mathbf{p}, (p_i + \epsilon)\mathbf{e}^i : i \in N\}, \mathbf{0}\right) .$$

Then $\mathbf{V}^\epsilon \subset \boldsymbol{\Delta}^N$, so by SMON and WPO, $\phi(\mathbf{V}^\epsilon) = \mathbf{p} = \phi^\mathbf{P}(\mathbf{V}^\epsilon)$. For every $\delta < 1$ there exists an ϵ with $\delta\alpha\mathbf{V}^\epsilon \subset \mathbf{S}$, where α is defined by $\alpha\mathbf{p} := \phi^\mathbf{P}(\mathbf{S})$. By SMON and HOM $\phi(\mathbf{S}) \geq \phi(\delta\alpha\mathbf{V}^\epsilon) = \delta\phi^\mathbf{P}(\mathbf{S})$. Letting $\delta \uparrow 1$, statement 1 follows. Statement 2 follows immediately from 1. To show 3, for $\beta \in \mathbb{R}$ with $\beta > 1$, let $\mathbf{S}^\beta := \text{com}(\mathbf{S} \cup \{\beta\phi^\mathbf{P}(\mathbf{S})\}, \mathbf{0})$. Then $\mathbf{S} \subset \mathbf{S}^\beta$, $\phi^\mathbf{P}(\mathbf{S}^\beta) \in P(\mathbf{S}^\beta)$. So by 2, $\phi^\mathbf{P}(\mathbf{S}^\beta) = \phi(\mathbf{S}^\beta)$, and by SMON, $\phi(\mathbf{S}) \leq \phi^\mathbf{P}(\mathbf{S}^\beta)$. Letting $\beta \downarrow 1$, Statement 3 follows. ■

If utility is monotonically increasing and profit is monotonically decreasing in w, then the solution can be calculated by setting the ratio of utility and profits equal to the ratio of the respective weights[2] and then solve for the wage:

$$\frac{U(w, L(w, \mathbf{q}), \mathbf{m})}{\pi(w, \mathbf{q})} = \frac{p_1}{p_2} = c\,. \tag{4.8}$$

If either union utility or profit is not monotonic, things are more complicated and it is important to investigate the shape of the bargaining set further.

4.4 Why the Proportional Solution?

An important question to begin with is the choice of the proportional solution as the proposed alternative. The number of proposed solution concepts in axiomatic bargaining game theory is quite large (see e.g. Peters, 1992) and the proportional solution is not even one of the most widely used in economics. It is not the aim here to discuss the implications of every solution for the wage bargaining problem. As argued in the introduction, the axioms that characterize the solution play an important role here and the discussion in this section emphasizes the importance of several axioms of the proportional solution in the union-firm context. However, there is a quite similar solution that has already been discussed in the union-firm context (see e.g. McDonald and Solow, 1981; Alexander, 1992; Alexander and Ledermann, 1996), the Kalai-Smorodinsky solution (KSS) (Kalai and Smorodinsky, 1975). This solution is a proportional solution where the weights are given by the respective aspiration level, i.e. the maximum attainable level of utility. Despite this seemingly minor difference, there are several reasons why the PS is more interesting. First, it does not suffer from the same lack of mathematical tractability mentioned by McDonald and Solow (1981) and Alexander (1992) concerning the KSS. As shown in chapter 6, it can lead to extremely simple wage equations. Second, as should be clear from the discussion in section 4.2, an important feature of bargaining sets in the right-to-manage model is not only the possible nonconvexity but also unboundedness. This implies that one of the parties does not have a finite aspiration level. The PS has the

[2] To assure existence it is necessary to make additional assumptions like: $\exists\, w_1$, $w_1 \leq \infty, \pi(w_1, \mathbf{q}) = 0$ and $\exists\, w_2, w_2 \geq 0, U(w_2, L(w_2, \mathbf{q}), \mathbf{m}) = 0$.

advantage, as shown in the previous section, that in contrast to the KSS it can handle these bargaining sets. Therefore it is applicable for virtually any possible combination of union and firm utilities, which makes it especially interesting. The most important point, however, is related to the axiomatic characterization. To keep the exposition concise, this is discussed together with the GNBS.

The most interesting axiom for the comparison of GNBS, KSS and PS is scale transformation covariance:

Scale Transformation Covariance (STC): For every $(\mathbf{S}, \mathbf{d}) \in \Sigma^N$ and all $\mathbf{a}, \mathbf{b} \in \mathbb{R}^N$, $\mathbf{a} \gg \mathbf{0}$ and $(\mathbf{aS} + \mathbf{b}, \mathbf{ad} + \mathbf{b}) \in \Sigma^N$, $\phi(\mathbf{aS} + \mathbf{b}, \mathbf{ad} + \mathbf{b}) = \mathbf{a}\phi(\mathbf{S}, \mathbf{d}) + \mathbf{b}$

which is fulfilled by the GNBS and the KSS, but not by the PS. If the parties have von Neumann-Morgenstern utility functions, the axiom ensures that only preferences and not the representation of these preferences influence the solution. This seems to be a good property on theoretical grounds, because no cardinal utility concept or interpersonal utility comparison is used. However, as discussed below, this property is not supported by empirical evidence. This result seems to have not been considered important enough to question the application of the GNBS to the union-firm bargain in the past.

This property implies that an increase in profit/utility, due to an increase in some exogenous factor, does not influence the solution, as long as the increase is of the multiplicative form. This holds for the KSS because the weight of this proportional solution is the aspiration level and this level is scaled by the same factor. If one takes a look at equation (4.8) it should be clear that in this case a proportional solution is not affected. But the increase in profit/utility is equivalent to an enlargement of the allocation set and, as was emphasized by Kalai (1977), should, in a "fair" solution, lead to an improvement for both parties. This is implied by SMON, a property of the PS. Especially in the union-firm context this notion of fairness seems to play a very important role, or it does so at least in the rhetoric of the bargaining parties. It is hard to believe that such an increase in e.g. profits would really not be of importance for the bargained wage.

The issue of fairness is often emphasized with regard to another property of the Nash solution, the independence of irrelevant alternatives axiom:

Independence of Irrelevant Alternatives (IIA): For all $(\mathbf{S}, \mathbf{d}), (\mathbf{T}, \mathbf{d}) \in \Sigma^N$ with $\mathbf{S} \subset \mathbf{T}$ and $\phi(\mathbf{T}, \mathbf{d}) \in \mathbf{S}$, $\phi(\mathbf{S}, \mathbf{d}) = \phi(\mathbf{T}, \mathbf{d})$

Intuitively this property implies that cutting off a piece of the bargaining set that does not contain the current solution does not change the solution. This is regarded as problematic by McDonald and Solow (1981) who argue that: "Intuitions about 'bargaining power' and 'fairness' might include the notion that if A *could* win a lot in a bargaining situation, he or she is 'entitled' to more than if he or she could only, in the best of circumstances, win a little" (p. 905f.). Since the KSS does not have this property, this solution is also suggested as an alternative by Alexander (1992). While this is not unreasonable, how much more important must it be when one of the parties is *really* winning more because the bargaining set changes. If fairness is an issue in wage bargaining, the axiom that is more important is STC and not IIA. Since the KSS fulfills STC, it is not further discussed here. Insofar the arguments below against the GNBS rely on this property, they are also arguments against the use of the KSS.

This property has been tested in several studies (for a survey see Roth and Malouf, 1979), a classic example being the study by Nydegger and Owen (1975). The players in the study had to divide a bunch of chips between them that could be exchanged in money after the bargain at certain given rates. A redistribution of the money after the bargain was not possible. This is the same situation as one often finds in the union-firm bargain when the bargain is on a level higher than the firm level. Here, the parties cannot e.g. lower wages to give more of the cake to the firm and then redistribute through another channel.[3] What happens if the exchange rate is changed for one of the parties? According to the study, this influences the bargain and the party that had to face a reduction in the exchange rate gets more in the bargain.[4] As already noted, this is implied by SMON. The GNBS can explain this result only under the assumption of quite special utilities. Let's denote the amount of chips with x and the exchange rate with e. Then the utility of player one U_1 will depend on the money he gets from the bargain:

$$U_1 = U_1(ex) . \tag{4.9}$$

As shown below, the bargaining outcome only reacts to exogenous factors if the elasticity of the utility does. This might be the case, but this is not a general property of the GNBS and it is indeed not satisfied for the frequently used Cobb-Douglas utility function. This makes the application of the GNBS to this problem questionable.

In contrast to the studies of Alexander (1992) and Alexander and Ledermann (1996), where the focus is on the comparison of the outcome of wage bargaining under different solutions, I want to emphasize the different comparative statics of the solutions here.

---

[3] In the bargain on the firm level this may be possible. It depends on what the purpose really is. If a high wage tax is to be avoided then it might be possible to redistribute the money from lower wages in form of fringe benefits that may be tax exempt.

[4] Actually, all the parties split the chips in such a way that the monetary payoffs after exchanging the chips for money were equal. This would be the prediction of the egalitarian solution under identical utilities, which is just a special case of the PS.

For the GNBS the comparative statics depend on how certain elasticities react to changes in the exogenous factors:

$$\frac{\partial w}{\partial \mathbf{q}} = -\frac{\frac{\partial \epsilon_{U w}}{\partial \mathbf{q}} - \frac{1-\chi}{\chi}\frac{\partial \epsilon_{\pi w}}{\partial \mathbf{q}}}{\frac{\partial \epsilon_{U w}}{\partial w} - \frac{1-\chi}{\chi}\frac{\partial \epsilon_{\pi w}}{\partial w}} \tag{4.10}$$

$$\frac{\partial w}{\partial \mathbf{m}} = -\frac{\frac{\partial \epsilon_{U w}}{\partial \mathbf{m}}}{\frac{\partial \epsilon_{U w}}{\partial w} - \frac{1-\chi}{\chi}\frac{\partial \epsilon_{\pi w}}{\partial w}} \; . \tag{4.11}$$

In light of the uncertainty concerning the functional form of profit or union utility functions, this result reduces sharply the informative content of this model. The PS has the following comparative statics:

$$\frac{\partial w}{\partial \mathbf{q}} = -\frac{\frac{\partial U}{\partial L}\frac{\partial L}{\partial \mathbf{q}} - c\frac{\partial \pi}{\partial \mathbf{q}}}{\frac{\partial U}{\partial w} - c\frac{\partial \pi}{\partial w}} \tag{4.12}$$

$$\frac{\partial w}{\partial \mathbf{m}} = -\frac{\frac{\partial U}{\partial \mathbf{m}}}{\frac{\partial U}{\partial w} - c\frac{\partial \pi}{\partial w}} \; . \tag{4.13}$$

As can be seen, the denominator is positive. Variables that increase profit generally increase the wage; variables that increase union utility decrease the wage. The effects are not clear for the **q** variables when

$$\operatorname{sign}(\partial L/\partial q_i) = \operatorname{sign}(\partial \pi/\partial q_i) \; . \tag{4.14}$$

Factors increasing (decreasing) profit can also increase (decrease) labour demand and therefore utility, which makes the net effect ambiguous. This remaining ambiguity can only be resolved by putting more structure on the problem, like with the GNBS. Nonetheless, the ambiguity is clearly reduced by the PS.

This delivers an important argument for the PS on methodological grounds. For any kind of empirical test it is clear that the PS is the more interesting hypothesis, because the PS is the more "improbable model" in the sense of Popper (1972). It has a larger set of empirically testable implications. The GNBS can only produce an equivalent amount of testable implications if the utilities are specified. But these utilities are not known with certainty. Therefore, when empirical analysis would reject an implication of the model, the theory can easily be "immunized" by changing the functional forms of the utilities. This suggests that as long as the model with the PS cannot be rejected, this should be the preferred model.

The most important example for a different behaviour of the model with the PS for this book is a proportional tax. For the firm, a proportional tax is actually nothing else than the exchange rate for one of the parties in the study of Nydegger and Owen. As discussed above such a tax would have no consequences on the bargained wage under the GNBS.

With the firm utility that is generally used this can easily be seen from the Nash maximand

$$\Omega = ((1 - \bar{t})\pi)^{1-\chi}(U)^{\chi} , \tag{4.15}$$

where a profit tax $\bar{t}$ does not influence the maximizing wage. Under the PS, in contrast, it would clearly be of importance and a higher profit tax would lower wages and increase employment because the employment decision is not influenced by this tax. Later in chapter 6 it is assumed that the firm utility is given by capital income, and this result will extend to the case of proportional capital income taxation under certain assumptions.

A further implication of STC is that in the case of technological progress or an increase of the capital stock, the GNBS implies no effect on wages in the case of a Cobb-Douglas profit function and a utility function that is multiplicatively separable in L. This can easily be verified in (3.11): the elasticity of profit and of labour demand with respect to the wage is constant in this case, and therefore the wage is not affected. This was noted by Manning (1993). He concludes that: "the theoretical arguments for the inclusion of productivity variables in wage equations are weak" (p. 108). This issue is of great importance for the application of the model. If the variables cancel out of the wage equation, the model can serve as an explanation for the observed wage stickiness over the business cycle, as discussed by McDonald and Solow (1981). A problem with this approach is that this is not very realistic in the long run, because wages finally adjust to productivity changes. Now consider the example of section 4.2 with union utility $U = (1 - \rho)wL^{\gamma}$ and a firm with Cobb-Douglas technology. Using the PS, the reduced form wage and employment equations for $\gamma \neq 1$ are given by:

$$w = Az^{\frac{1-\gamma}{1-\gamma+\delta(1-\gamma)}} \tag{4.16}$$

$$L = \delta a A^{-\delta-1} , \tag{4.17}$$

where A depends on δ, a, γ, ρ and c. Employment does not depend on z, and therefore the PS delivers an explanation of the long run behaviour of wages and employment for this utility. A further discussion of this point is given in chapter 6.

Finally, practical considerations also support the PS. In the concrete bargaining situation it is clearly easier for the parties to evaluate the impact of a wage increase on profits than on the elasticity of profit with respect to the wage. The same reasoning should hold for some well-defined measure of union utility. It therefore seems reasonable that a solution concept like the PS is easier to implement and therefore more practical than the GNBS. This makes it more plausible as a description of the bargaining outcome.

4.5 An Evaluation of Arguments Against the Proportional Solution

A point that can be made against the PS is that it is only weakly Pareto optimal, while the GNBS is strongly Pareto optimal. For the union-firm bargain this property is indeed problematic and not convincing if the solution is in fact not Pareto optimal. This might be the case if e.g. the union utility is not monotonically increasing in the wage, and there exists a maximum wage that would be chosen by the monopoly union. In this case it is possible that the bargaining outcome implies a utility for the firm that is less than the utility it would get from the monopoly union wage. This implies that the firm actually has to throw away a part of its profit, as is illustrated in figure 4.3, which is certainly not plausible. In this case one would expect the outcome to be simply the monopoly union wage, which is the Pareto optimal point denoted by ϕ^{mu}. The PS can easily be extended in this way as is shown in chapter 5.

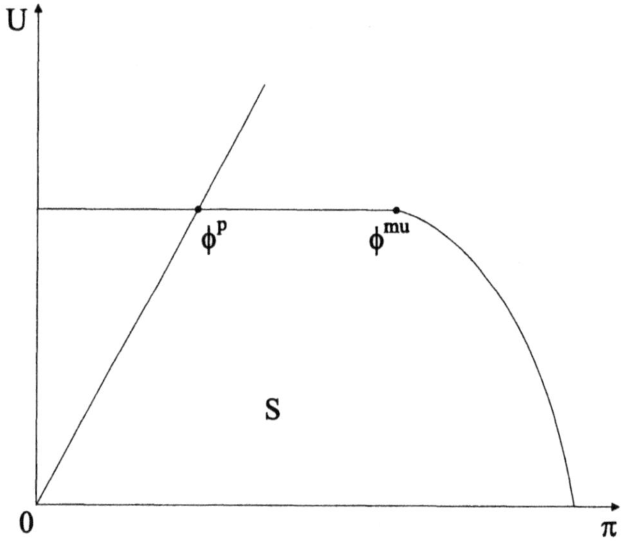

Fig. 4.3. A Pareto inefficient PS

It is sometimes seen as problematic that the solution is not fully determined because the weights are not specified. This is clearly a disadvantage if one is interested in a numerical solution for fully specified utility functions. If one is only interested in comparative statics, as theoretical economists generally are, this is not of importance. It is sufficient to assume that there are some weights that pin down the solution. For empirical studies, like the one in this book, it is also not important because the ratio of the weights can be estimated along with the other variables. In this respect it is even an advantage, because a possible misspecification of a utility by a multiplicative factor is simply corrected by a multiplicative transformation of the weight of the respective bargaining party with the same factor (Kalai, 1977) and the elasticities of the bargaining solution with respect to exogenous variables will still be estimated correctly.

A final criticism might be the case of a rich and a poor person bargaining over an amount of money. If the net utilities are split equally between the parties the rich one would get much more money out of the bargain than the poor, because one should assume that his marginal utility is lower, which seems to run counter to the notion of fairness invoked at several points of the discussion. But with unspecified weights the PS does not imply an equal sharing rule and, as mentioned above, the emphasis in the whole discussion is not on a forecast of the numerical outcome of the bargain, but to find a model with plausible comparative statics in the union-firm bargain. And whatever the weights for the bargain in this example may be, when the rich person gets richer he will get less and when the poor person gets poorer he will get more and vice versa. In *this* respect the fairness is secured by the PS.

This ends the theoretical discussion of bargaining models. Evidence on the relevance of this discussion for wage bargaining in Germany is given in the empirical part of the book. Before commencing with an empirical application of the model using West German data, however, some evidence is given in the next chapter that unemployment in Germany is really caused by union-firm bargaining and not by some other possible source of wage rigidity.

5. Labour Market Models and Wage Dynamics

The trade union model is not the only candidate for the explanation of permanent involuntary unemployment. One of the most important class of models proposed in the literature is the efficiency wage model.[1] In the textbook by Blanchard and Fischer (1989) efficiency wage theory is said to be "one of the most promising directions of research at this stage" (p. 463). In these models it is profitable for firms to increase the wage above the market clearing wage, generally because it increases the productivity of the workers. In efficiency wage models of the shirking variant (Calvo, 1979; Shapiro and Stiglitz, 1984; Bowles, 1985) the workers cannot be perfectly monitored and therefore they have an incentive to shirk on the job. In this case it can be profitable for the firm to increase wages when this leads to less shirking of the workers. When the wage rises above the average wage in the economy, it becomes more costly for workers to shirk. Shirkers risk detection, and getting fired now implies an income loss even if one immediately finds another job. If all firms increase their wages, involuntary unemployment will result, introducing an additional cost of losing the job for workers, because with some probability they will end up on the dole. In equilibrium it is not profitable for a firm to increase its wage further at the given unemployment rate, because the productivity enhancing effect no longer compensates the additional costs. A similar story can be told for turnover costs when higher wages lead to less fluctuation, as in the models of Stiglitz (1974) and Salop (1979), and for adverse selection, where the average productivity of a worker in the pool of job applicants is correlated with the offered real wage (Weiss, 1980). A mechanism that relies on "fairness" in an even stronger sense than the bargaining model of the previous chapter is introduced by the gift exchange hypothesis of Akerlof (1982). The idea is that the workers are willing to increase their effort above a given minimum level if they think that the wage is a "fair" wage. This amounts to an exchange of the gift effort for the gift higher wages. In this section I do not go into the details of any of these models, and the idea of efficiency wages is captured with a simple effort parameter that depends on the wage and increases effective labour input in the production function of the firm. This was suggested by Solow (1979).

[1] For a survey see Weiss (1991).

In light of the number of different possible reasons for efficiency wages, the obvious question is why union-firm bargaining should be the more likely cause of German unemployment. Since the efficiency wage model and the bargaining model have very different implications for economic policy, it is clearly very important to discriminate between the two.[2] This chapter tries to make some progress in this respect by analyzing the interaction between actual wages and contract wages.

In section 5.1 a unified framework of wage negotiation is developed, in which an efficiency wage regime and a bargaining regime can be identified. From this model one can draw conclusions about the nature of causation that should be observable between actual and contract wages in both regimes, which is done in section 5.2. This is used to discriminate between the regimes in a seasonal error correction model in section 5.3. The last section concludes.

5.1 A Unified Framework

In this section a model is derived that incorporates the efficiency wage model as a special case of a more general bargaining model. The only difference to the standard model, discussed in chapter 3, lies in the introduction of effort. The profit of the firm is now given by

$$\pi = \pi(w, \mathbf{q}, e(w, \mathbf{j})) , \tag{5.1}$$

where $e(w, \mathbf{j})$ is the effort function that depends on the wage and a vector of other variables $\mathbf{j}$ with $e_w > 0, e_{ww} < 0$. The vector $\mathbf{j}$ generally includes alternative wages, nonlabour income, unemployment etc. As before, the fallback point is zero and $\bar{r}$ is defined as

$$\pi(\bar{r}, \mathbf{q}, e(\bar{r}, \mathbf{j})) = 0 . \tag{5.2}$$

The corresponding labour demand curve is given by

$$L = L(w, \mathbf{q}, e(w, \mathbf{j})) . \tag{5.3}$$

Since effort rises with the wage, there might be a range of wages where it is profitable for the firm to raise wages for all employees to elicit more effort and thereby increase output. It is assumed that the efficiency wage that maximizes profits is given by

$$\bar{w} = \underset{w}{\operatorname{argmax}}\, \pi(w, \mathbf{q}, e(w, \mathbf{j})) . \tag{5.4}$$

[2] As discussed by Manning (1995b), in an efficiency wage equilibrium it is not even clear whether lower real wages would really lead to more employment.

As before, the union is assumed to have utility

$$U = U(w, L(w, \mathbf{q}, e(w, \mathbf{j})), \mathbf{m}) \tag{5.5}$$

and reservation wage r^*, defined as

$$U(r^*, L(r^*, \mathbf{q}, e(r^*, \mathbf{j})), \mathbf{m}) = 0 \; . \tag{5.6}$$

The monopoly union wage in this case is given by

$$w^* = \operatorname*{argmax}_{w} U(w, L(w, \mathbf{q}, e(w, \mathbf{j})), \mathbf{m}) \; . \tag{5.7}$$

It is assumed that the following inequalities hold: $r^* < \bar{w} < w^* < \bar{r}$.

The first inequality is a reasonable result in efficiency wage models. In many specifications of union utility, the reservation wage of the union coincides with the reservation wage of the individual worker. For the firm it is profitable to raise wages above this individual reservation wage. In the model of Shapiro and Stiglitz (1984) for instance, the worker shirks if the wage paid by the firm is equal to the reservation wage, and the efficiency wage is therefore always above the reservation wage in this model. The relation between the monopoly union wage and the efficiency wage is discussed by Bulkley and Myles (1996). In most cases the assumption made here coincides with the result of the theoretical model. The monopoly union sets wages above the efficiency wage. The last inequality is only for expositional purposes—to include all possible cases—and not of importance for the following discussion.

Given these definitions it is possible to derive the allocation set of all possible combinations of π and U for different wages. This set is given by $\mathbf{A} = \{\mathbf{x} \in \mathbb{R}^2 \mid \mathbf{x} = (U, \pi) \text{ for } r^* \leq w \leq \bar{r}\}$. If free disposability of profit/utility is assumed the set can be extended to $\mathbf{S} = \{\mathbf{y} \in \mathbb{R}^2 \mid \mathbf{y} \leq \mathbf{x}, \mathbf{x} \in \mathbf{A}\}$. The allocation set is drawn in figure 5.1. For simplicity it is assumed in the figure that the bargaining set is convex. The solutions given by the wages $\bar{w}$ and w^* are indicated by ϕ^{ew} and ϕ^{mu} respectively. The set of strictly Pareto optimal solutions is given by $P(\mathbf{S}) = \{\mathbf{x} \in \mathbf{A} \mid \mathbf{x} = (U, \pi) \text{ for } \bar{w} \leq w \leq w^*\}$. In the figure one can identify three different regimes that are possible and are numbered from 1 to 3. It should be noted that the free disposability assumption makes outcomes possible where the wage is set to either $\bar{w}$ or w^* and one party disposes part of its utility.

The important question is whether the bargaining outcome is equal to or below the efficiency wage, as in regime 1, or whether it is above the efficiency wage, as in regimes 2 and 3. The first case is called efficiency wage regime, because in this regime actual wages would be determined by efficiency wage considerations. Only in the other two regimes would the minimum wage nature of contract wages be binding, and a bargaining model would be the appropriate model of wage setting. It might be that even in these regimes it is not innocuous to neglect effort considerations, as is generally done in standard bargaining models, but this is clearly less problematic than using such

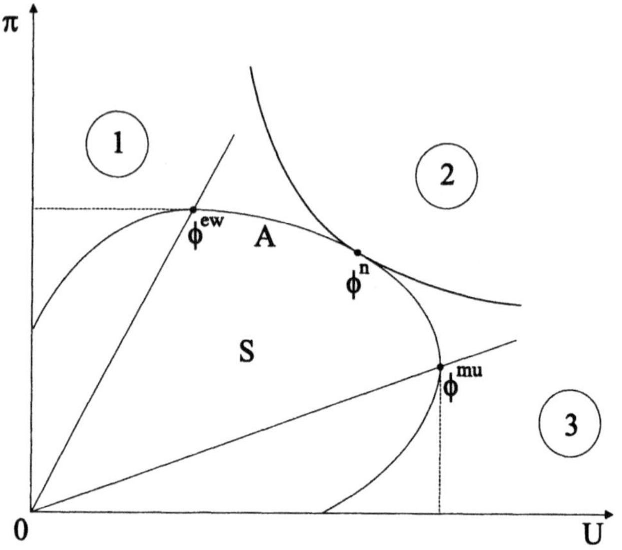

Fig. 5.1. Unified model

a model for the explanation of actual wages if one is in the efficiency wage regime. Therefore, a first task is to develop a test of regime discriminating between these two cases. This, at least, would be the first impression from the model so far.

However, on second sight, it is not clear that in a bargaining model with non-negligible trade union power the efficiency wage is a possible outcome. The traditionally used Nash bargaining solution, where the bargained wage maximizes

$$\Omega = (\pi(w, \mathbf{q}, e(w, \mathbf{j})))^{1-\chi}(U(w, L(w, \mathbf{q}, e(w, \mathbf{j})), \mathbf{m})^{\chi} \qquad \chi \in [0, 1], \qquad (5.8)$$

is depicted by ϕ^n in figure 5.1. As should be clear from the diagram, the contract wage is always above the efficiency wage with this solution. The efficiency wage would only be the solution in a situation where $\chi = 0$ and the union does not have any bargaining power. Therefore, the empirical test that is done below would amount to a test of $\chi = 0$ vs $\chi \neq 0$ in this model. A powerless union is clearly a rather extreme situation, especially in Germany, and one might conclude from this argument that an efficiency wage regime is something that is rarely of much practical importance.

This result contrasts with a strand of literature that sees efficiency wages at the center of the European unemployment problem. The analysis by Phelps (1994), for example, concentrates solely on efficiency wage models to explain the recent cycles in employment and output in Europe. One should therefore conclude that a situation where efficiency wages are above contract wages is not considered as an improbable event by many economists. Interestingly, a simple modification of the proportional solution, introduced in the previous chapter, leads to a fundamentally different result compared to the model with the Nash solution.

Using the proportional solution, the bargained wage $\hat{w}$ is determined by

$$\frac{U(\hat{w}, L(\hat{w}, \mathbf{q}, e(\hat{w}, \mathbf{j})), \mathbf{m})}{\pi(\hat{w}, \mathbf{q}, e(\hat{w}, \mathbf{j}))} = c\,. \tag{5.9}$$

As mentioned earlier, a drawback of this solution is that the wage could be not Pareto optimal. In the bargaining framework developed above, this would be the case for $\hat{w} < \bar{w}$ or $\hat{w} > w^*$. It seems implausible that such a wage would result from the bargaining process. The weakly Pareto optimal solution, where the solution would be $\bar{w}$ for $\hat{w} < \bar{w}$ and w^* for $\hat{w} > w^*$, but one of the players disposes part of his utility to keep the solution proportional, is theoretically possible but is hardly of any practical relevance.[3] It seems more plausible that in those cases the Pareto optimal solutions given by ϕ^{ew} and ϕ^{mu} are the result of the bargaining. This idea corresponds to the solution E introduced by Roth (1979). Since this is a modification of the egalitarian solution, which is equivalent to the proportional solution for $c = 1$, it is necessary to rescale the utility of one party appropriately before applying the solution. The proportional solution can be rewritten as

$$\frac{U(\hat{w}, L(\hat{w}, \mathbf{q}, e(\hat{w}, \mathbf{j})), \mathbf{m})}{c\pi(\hat{w}, \mathbf{q}, e(\hat{w}, \mathbf{j}))} = 1\,, \tag{5.10}$$

and is therefore identical to the egalitarian solution for union utility U and firm utility $\bar{\pi} = c\pi$. This leads to the transformed allocation set $\bar{\mathbf{S}}$ defined accordingly and its Pareto optimal subset given by $P(\bar{\mathbf{S}})$.

The solution E is defined as: $E(\bar{\mathbf{S}}) = \mathbf{x} \in P(\bar{\mathbf{S}})$ such that $\min(x_1, x_2) > \min(y_1, y_2)$ for all $\mathbf{y} \in P(\bar{\mathbf{S}})$ such that $\mathbf{y} \neq \mathbf{x}$. A characterization of this solution is given in Roth (1979). In regime 1 the wage that is given by the proportional solution is smaller than the efficiency wage. In this case the solution E picks the efficiency wage as bargaining solution. In the second regime the bargained wage is in the interval $\bar{w} < \hat{w} < w^*$. This corresponds to the outcome of the proportional solution. In the third regime the proportional solution would imply a wage $\hat{w} > w^*$. The solution E therefore leads to the monopoly union wage. In this model it is not unlikely to be in the first regime. A test of regime as developed below is therefore interesting because there is no strong a priori argument that would exclude regime 1 as an outcome.

[3] However, one could argue that the union and the firm generally bargain not only over the wage but also about working conditions, working time, holidays, sickness pay etc. The bargaining parties could use these things to achieve a redistribution that would mimic such a disposal of utility. For this purpose it would be necessary to use this instrument for a shift in the bargaining set such that the outcome of the proportional solution coincides with the efficiency wage or the monopoly union wage. Possible changes in the efficiency and the monopoly union wage itself caused by this measure have to be considered, of course.

Further, it should be noted that a change in regime is not possible under the Nash solution through changes in the **q**, **j** or **m** variables, but only through a quite dramatic change of bargaining power, or, in the game theoretic interpretation (Binmore et al., 1986), of time preference. In the model presented above, however, we can think of regime changes as not only driven by c, but also by changes in technological progress, taxation, output and factor prices, replacement ratios etc. This makes a change in regime an event that is the result of the usual macroeconomic shocks that are the subject of our theoretical and empirical models. In this sense the model is a step forward towards the integration of the two theories in a common framework of wage determination. The same holds for the monopoly union model.

However, for the argument that follows, it is not necessary to believe in this quite special solution. It is sufficient to accept that an efficiency wage regime is a possible scenario for wage setting in Germany and that it is interesting to test for it. An obvious way of doing this would be to test whether the variables **m** that influence only union utility are influencing contract wages or not. This should only be the case under regimes 2 and 3. However, there is clearly a problem with such an approach since many of these variables, e.g. consumer prices, wage taxes, the replacement ratio etc., are also likely to be elements of the vector **j** influencing effort and therefore profit. It is not clear in this case if such a test is really convincing. There also exists already a large literature on this topic,[4] where it is shown that these variables have an influence on the wage and it is questionable whether an additional study in this direction would lead to new insights. Therefore, a different strategy is pursued in this chapter.

In regime 1 the contract wage is either connected to the efficiency wage, as in the model with the solution E, or it may be an irrelevant minimum wage that is set independently of the efficiency wage. The discussion in the next section will focus on the first case, where the determinants of the efficiency wage are also the determinants of the contract wage. If the efficiency wage changes this induces a similar change of the contract wage in the next wage round and this forms the basis of the empirical argument. I return to the second case in section 5.3.

5.2 An Empirical Implication

The empirical discrimination is based on the implications of the different regimes for the dynamic interaction between actual wages w_t and contract wages cw_t in West Germany. The analysis uses the following simple argument. Generally, wage bargaining in Germany takes place only once a year. If we are in an efficiency wage regime, then we would expect that any shock that

[4] For surveys of the empirical literature on union-firm bargaining see Holmlund (1989) and Booth (1995).

drives up the efficiency wage of the firms during the year leads to rising actual wages since the contract wage represents only a minimum wage. The efficiency wage that has emerged at the end of the year will determine the new contract wage. The change in actual wages that one observes in the quarters before the new wage agreement should therefore help in forecasting the change in contract wages in this regime. If, by contrast, the efficiency wage of the firms is well below the contract wage, this is not necessarily the case. The firms do not have an incentive to change wages and all shocks would only change employment as in the standard model with fixed wages. Therefore, in a VAR framework, Granger causality of actual wages in the contract wage equation can be seen as a necessary condition to be in regime 1. This argument is intuitive and should hold under quite general conditions.

Of course, there is a problem of asymmetry in this argument caused by the minimum wage nature of the contract wage. If a firm pays the contract wage at a certain point in time, e.g. immediately after the contract wage was renegotiated, only positive shocks that increase the efficiency wage of the firm can change the actual wage. Negative shocks would fall fully on employment; the actual wage would not change and could not serve as an indicator of future contract wages. A standard VAR model does not capture this property and would therefore be inappropriate. However, this problem is substantially less of importance when the bargaining takes place between a union and an employers association representing a large number of diverse firms as is the case in Germany. If firms differ regarding their efficiency wage, then the asymmetry argument holds only for the firms with efficiency wages near the contract wage. If this number is small, then the problem is negligible. This is discussed in more detail in the appendix to this chapter.

To get a clearer impression of the idea it is helpful to build a small stylized model of the interaction of the two wages. The average contract wage changes in each quarter of the year, because in a part $k = 1, 2, 3, 4$ of the economy the contract wages are renegotiated. Therefore, it is assumed that the quarterly growth rate of the average contract wage $\hat{cw}_t$ is a function of the yearly contract wage growth $\bar{cw}_t^k$ in the respective part of the economy:

$$\hat{cw}_t = f(\bar{cw}_t^k) \quad f' > 0\,, \tag{5.11}$$

with

$$\bar{cw}_t^k = \frac{cw_t^k - cw_{t-4}^k}{cw_{t-4}^k}\,. \tag{5.12}$$

In an efficiency wage regime, this growth rate itself depends on the shocks u_t^k that drive the efficiency wage of the sector k according to

$$\bar{cw}_t^k = \sum_{i=1}^{4} u_{t-i}^k\,. \tag{5.13}$$

These shocks also drive the quarterly growth rate of the actual wage in each period

$$\hat{w}_t = p \left(\sum_{k=1}^{4} u_t^k \right) , \tag{5.14}$$

where p is some proportionality factor. Solving equation (5.14) for the shocks that are influencing the contract wage and substituting in equation (5.13) gives

$$c\bar{w}_t^k = \frac{1}{p} \sum_{i=1}^{4} \hat{w}_{t-i} - \sum_{j=1}^{4} \sum_{l \neq k} u_{t-j}^l . \tag{5.15}$$

This establishes a dependence of the contract wage growth on the actual wage growth in earlier periods.[5] The actual wage growth is only a noisy signal and correlated with the error term of the equation. Nonetheless, It should be useful for predicting contract wage growth. I return to this point later.

Of course, there are other reasons why there might be a Granger causality from actual to contract wages. A simple argument is that contract wages are only minimum wages, and there is scope for market determined wages above the minimum wage, especially in times of low unemployment. Given that unemployment is not spread equally over the different regions, sectors and occupations it could even be of importance in times of high unemployment because of partial shortages, but the effect is likely to be much smaller. These wages will react to any change in labour market conditions. If the amount of market determined wages is large, then actual wages should be good indicators for future contract wages, because the changes in labour market conditions generally affect contract wages in the same way.

The main difference between this argument and the efficiency wage theory is, therefore, that it should be of relevance only in times of low unemployment, while the efficiency wage theory leads to Granger causality of actual wages even in times of high unemployment, insofar efficiency wages are the cause of it. This will be of importance in the empirical analysis that follows.

5.3 Empirical Results

For the analysis of the dynamic interactions of different time series the natural starting point is a VAR. I apply the model to the growth rates of the two

[5] If the shocks in different sectors are correlated then past contract wage growth in one sector would also be important for forecasting contract wage growth in another sector. This would complicate the model. Since the lagged contract wage is not significant in the important part of the empirical analysis the issue is neglected here.

wages, measured as the first difference of the natural logarithms, as in the model of the last section.[6] This choice also fits best to the seasonal cointegration framework that is used to describe the dynamic structure of the data as will be shown subsequently. The series used are aggregate data for West Germany and have been supplied by the DIW.

Before starting with the analysis of the joint dynamics of the series, the seasonal properties of the data are derived in a univariate framework. This is necessary to arrive at an appropriate dynamic specification. Two tests are applied for this purpose, the HEGY test (Hylleberg et al., 1990) and the CH test (Canova and Hansen, 1995) as discussed in the methods chapter. The results of the HEGY test are given in table 5.1.

Table 5.1. HEGY tests

	t-tests		F-test
	$\pi_1 = 0$	$\pi_2 = 0$	$\pi_3 = \pi_4 = 0$
$\Delta \ln cw_t[3]$	-2.91^*	-1.80	5.66^*
$\Delta \ln w_t[5]$	-2.37	-1.66	1.61

* 10% sig., ** 5% sig.

The results indicate that at the ten percent significance level the growth rate of contract wages is stationary at the zero frequency and frequency $\pi/2$, but has a seasonal unit root at the frequency π. The growth rate of actual wages, in contrast, seems to have a unit root at all frequencies. This differing behaviour of the series, especially at the zero frequency, would be rather surprising.

In a first step the results on the seasonal unit roots are checked by the mentioned CH test that is applied to the second differences of the data. The results in table 5.2 show that both series have all seasonal unit roots. The conflicting evidence necessitates a decision which test to follow. I decided to follow the CH test in this case and apply the filter $1 + L + L^2 + L^3$ that removes all seasonal unit roots to both series. The results of the seasonal cointegration analysis that is done in the next step support this choice. A plot of the seasonally adjusted series is given in figure 5.2. Additional augmented Dickey-Fuller tests on the filtered series given in table 5.3 cannot reject the hypothesis that the growth rates of the series are integrated. Therefore, it is assumed that the filter $1 - L^4$ is necessary to make the series stationary.

[6] It should be noted that in the German literature on the relation between actual and contract wages (see Schnabel, 1994, for a survey) the role of measurement error is contentious. It is uncontroversial, however, that the levels of actual and contract wages are not measured in the same way. The wage drift, measured by the difference between the changes in actual and contract wages is seen as less misleading. This is one of the reasons why I concentrate solely on the relation between the growth rates of the two wages and neglect an analysis of the levels.

Table 5.2. CH tests

	unit-root tests	
	π	$\pi/2$
$\Delta^2 \ln cw_t$	4.54**	2.21**
$\Delta^2 \ln w_t$	7.16**	4.49**

* 10% sig., ** 5% sig.

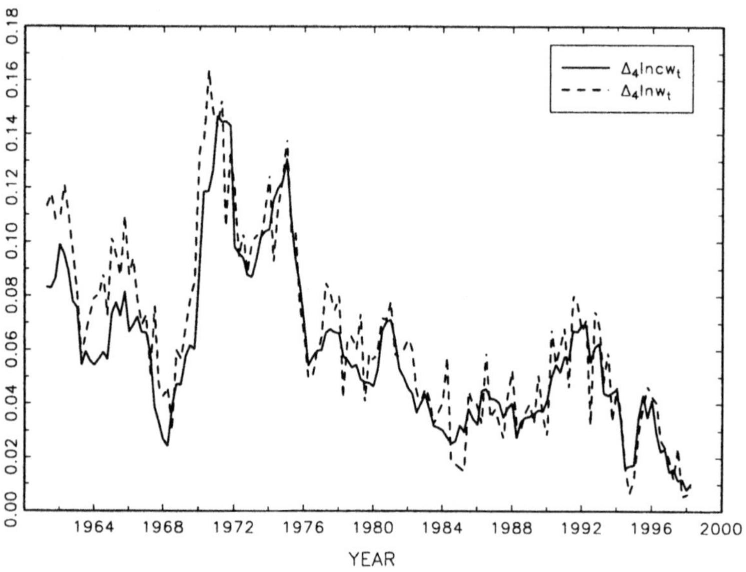

Fig. 5.2. Seasonally adjusted wage growth rates

Table 5.3. ADF test

	t-test	p-value
$\Delta_4 \ln cw_t$	−2.13	0.23
$\Delta_4 \ln w_t$	−1.70	0.43

With this information about the seasonal properties of the series it does not seem appropriate to apply a simple VAR to the quarterly growth rates. As shown by Toda and Phillips (1993) ignoring the existence of unit roots in the data can lead to biased inference on the significance of the estimated parameters. It is therefore necessary to take account of the unit roots in the dynamic model.

To determine the dynamic interactions between the variables the following Gaussian VAR(p) for the growth rates is assumed:

$$\boldsymbol{\Phi}(L)\mathbf{z}_t = \boldsymbol{\epsilon}_t \tag{5.16}$$

$$\boldsymbol{\Phi}(L) = \mathbf{I} - \boldsymbol{\Phi}_1 L - \boldsymbol{\Phi}_2 L^2 - \cdots - \boldsymbol{\Phi}_p L^p \tag{5.17}$$

for $t = 1, 2, \ldots, T$, where $\mathbf{z}_t = (\Delta \ln cw_t, \Delta \ln w_t)'$ and the $\boldsymbol{\epsilon}_t$ are n.i.i.d with mean zero and covariance matrix $\boldsymbol{\Sigma}$. This implies the following error correction representation of the VAR:

$$\begin{aligned}\Delta_4 \mathbf{z}_t = &\ \boldsymbol{\Pi}_1 \mathbf{y}_{1,t-1} + \boldsymbol{\Pi}_2 \mathbf{y}_{2,t-1} + \boldsymbol{\Pi}_3 \mathbf{y}_{3,t-1} + \boldsymbol{\Pi}_4 \mathbf{y}_{3,t} \\ &+ \mathbf{A}_1 \Delta_4 \mathbf{z}_{t-1} + \cdots + \mathbf{A}_{p-4} \Delta_4 \mathbf{z}_{t-p+4} + \boldsymbol{\epsilon}_t \ ,\end{aligned} \tag{5.18}$$

where

$$\mathbf{y}_{1,t} = (1 + L + L^2 + L^3)\mathbf{z}_t \tag{5.19}$$

$$\mathbf{y}_{2,t} = (1 - L + L^2 - L^3)\mathbf{z}_t \tag{5.20}$$

$$\mathbf{y}_{3,t} = (L - L^3)\mathbf{z}_t \tag{5.21}$$

and the $\boldsymbol{\Pi}_i$ and the $\mathbf{A}_i$ are functions of the $\boldsymbol{\Phi}_i$. In this framework it is possible to test for cointegration at the nonseasonal and the seasonal frequencies as demonstrated in Lee (1992).

The hypothesis of cointegration at the zero frequency, the frequency π and contemporaneous cointegration at the frequency $\pi/2$ are considered. In the ECM these hypothesis correspond to ranks $r > 0$ of the matrices $\boldsymbol{\Pi}_1$, $\boldsymbol{\Pi}_2$ and $\boldsymbol{\Pi}_3$ respectively. The restriction to contemporaneous cointegration at the annual frequency implies $\boldsymbol{\Pi}_4 = 0$ which seems to be a plausible assumption in the given framework. The lag length of the VAR is chosen by an AIC criterion. The results of the cointegration tests are given in table 5.4. The tests included a constant and seasonal dummies. The critical values are taken from Lee and Siklos (1995).

Table 5.4. Trace tests

H_0	$\boldsymbol{\Pi}_1$	$\boldsymbol{\Pi}_2$	$\boldsymbol{\Pi}_3$
r=0	45.76**	11.45	19.61
r=1	5.70	3.35	4.04

* 10% sig., ** 5% sig.

The results indicate that there is exactly one cointegration vector at the zero frequency and there is no cointegration at any of the seasonal frequencies. The maximum likelihood estimate of the cointegration vector is given by $(1, -0.86)$. This determines the equilibrium error: $x_t = \Delta_4 \ln cw_t - 0.86 * \Delta_4 \ln w_t$.

This result is strong evidence against a situation where the contract wage is an ineffective minimum wage that is not affected by changes in actual wages. This long-run relation can only be the result of either contract wages causing actual wages or actual wages causing contract wages or both.

In the next step the resulting ECM is estimated by OLS. For the full sample this leads to the estimates in table 5.5. To check for autocorrelation in the residuals, the test proposed by Durbin (1970) has been calculated and is reported in the last line.

Table 5.5. Estimation results 1961:2-1998:1

	Dependent variable	
	$\Delta_4 \Delta \ln cw_t$	$\Delta_4 \Delta \ln w_t$
x_{t-1}	-0.29^{**}	0.30^{**}
$\Delta_4 \Delta \ln cw_{t-1}$	0.33^{**}	0.65^{**}
$\Delta_4 \Delta \ln w_{t-1}$	-0.15^{**}	-0.40^{**}
Durbin's h	-0.80	-1.44

* 10% sig., ** 5% sig.

The results indicate that there is a two way causation between actual and contract wages. All parameters are significant, and the autocorrelation test does not reject the null hypothesis of no autocorrelation. Since unemployment is considerably lower in the first half than in the second half of the sample, the discussion in the last section suggests to test for a possible structural break in the equation for contract wages. For this purpose I calculated recursive residuals and the CUSUM test according to Brown et al. (1975) that are reported in figure 5.3. The bands are drawn for the 5% significance level. The CUSUM test is shown to be asymptotically valid even in the case of a dynamic regression in Krämer et al. (1988).

The test results suggest that there might be a structural break somewhere near 1972. Therefore, I split the sample at this date and reestimated the model for both samples. The results are given in table 5.6 and table 5.7. As can be seen, the dynamics differ substantially between the samples. In the first sample from 1961:3 to 1971:4 the causation still runs in both directions, while in the second sample from 1972:1 to 1998:1 the causation runs only in one direction from contract wages to actual wages. Additional regressions for other split dates later than 1972 lead to the same qualitative results. Durbin's h test does not indicate a dynamic misspecification in the equations.

In the next section the results are interpreted and the implications for the econometric modeling of the West German labour market are discussed.

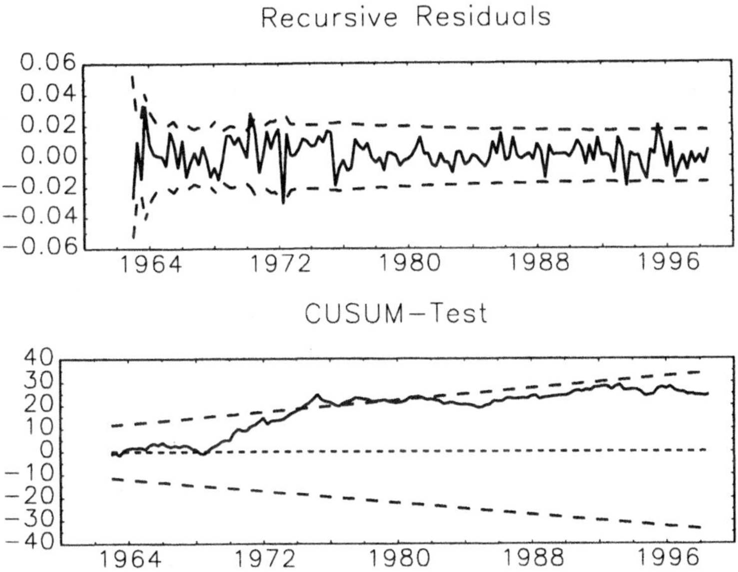

Fig. 5.3. Structural stability tests

Table 5.6. Estimation results 1961:3-1971:4

	Dependent variable	
	$\Delta_4 \Delta \ln cw_t$	$\Delta_4 \Delta \ln w_t$
x_{t-1}	-0.55^{**}	-0.05
$\Delta_4 \Delta \ln cw_{t-1}$	0.40^{**}	0.71^{**}
$\Delta_4 \Delta \ln w_{t-1}$	-0.30^{**}	-0.53^{**}
Durbin's h	0.38	0.09

* 10% sig., ** 5% sig.

Table 5.7. Estimation results 1972:1-1998:1

	Dependent variable	
	$\Delta_4 \Delta \ln cw_t$	$\Delta_4 \Delta \ln w_t$
x_{t-1}	-0.00	0.86^{**}
$\Delta_4 \Delta \ln cw_{t-1}$	0.15	0.41^{**}
$\Delta_4 \Delta \ln w_{t-1}$	-0.01	-0.19^{*}
Durbin's h	-0.32	-1.50

* 10% sig., ** 5% sig.

5.4 Conclusions

In light of the discussion in section 5.2 the results of the previous section are easy to interpret. While in the first sample from 1961:3-1971:4, with relatively low unemployment, the causation runs in both directions and therefore actual wages cause contract wages, this is not observed in the second sample with higher unemployment rates. This does not support the efficiency wage argument, at least in the second sample which is the more important one. If the unemployment that we observe after 1972 would be the result of efficiency wages then one should expect that changes in the actual wage are useful indicators of future contract wage growth. But this is not the case. A possible caveat to this reasoning would be that, as discussed in section 5.2, the actual wage is only a noisy signal, maybe too noisy. If this is true then it is not clear why the actual wage is not too noisy to help in forecasting the contract wage in the other sample. The first sample is much shorter and still the actual wage enters highly significant in the equation for the contract wage. Interestingly, the sample split coincides with a period of extremely large increases in nominal wages, as can be seen in figure 5.2, that have also lead to the largest increases in real wages in the observation period. This suggests that after these dramatic increases real wages were too high to make wage setting above contract wages worthwhile to employers.

Taken together, the results support a view of the labour market that gives wage bargaining (regime 2) or union wage setting (regime 3) a central role in the explanation of the development of actual wages and therefore unemployment in West Germany. Contract wages seem to be the driving force behind the growth in actual wage. As a consequence, any macroeconomic policy that aims at reducing unemployment in Germany should be evaluated with regard to its effects in a union-firm bargaining model and not on the basis of efficiency wage models. It is this line of labour market theory that will form the basis of the subsequent chapters that try to shed some light on the causes of the high German unemployment rate in the last decades.

5.5 Appendix

This appendix discusses why the mentioned problem of asymmetry is of minor importance for Germany where the bargaining takes place with an employers association representing a large number of diverse firms. Assume that the firms that are represented by the employers association differ in their efficiency wage, e.g. because of different monitoring technologies, and that there is a continuum of firms distributed equally on the interval $[0, 1]$ with density $f(x) = 1$. For expositional simplicity I assume that each firm has the same fixed number of identical employees normalized to one. There is an associated wage function $ew_t = ew_t(x), ew_t' > 0$ that represents the efficiency wage of each firm at time t on the unit interval. The wage that is the bargaining outcome in regime 1 is assumed to be the wage of the median voter given by $cw_t = ew_{t-1}(0.5)$.[7] The average actual wage will be higher than this wage, because the firms with efficiency wages higher than the bargained wage will pay their efficiency wage.[8] This is possible because the contract wage is only a minimum wage. In the same period there is a shock to the economy s_t that moves the wage function either upward or downward leading to the after-shock wage function ew_t with inverse g_t. This function determines the average actual wage in this period given by

$$w_t = cw_t + \int_{g_t(cw_t)}^{1} (ew_t(x) - cw_t)dx \; . \tag{5.22}$$

Since contract wages are not renegotiated every period, any shocks in the intermediate periods are reflected only in the actual wage. After i periods wages are renegotiated and the new contract wage is given by

$$cw_{t+i} = ew_{t+i-1}(0.5) \; . \tag{5.23}$$

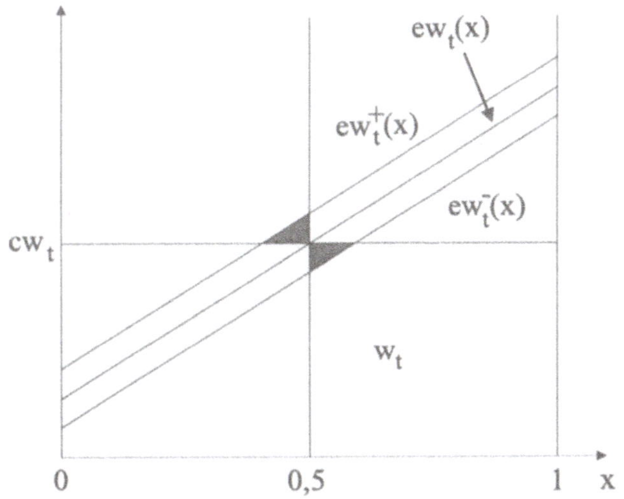

Fig. 5.4. Wage functions

[7] This assumption is not crucial, however, as will become clear later.

[8] The model is therefore a possible explanation for the wage gap between actual wages and contract wages observed in Germany. As discussed by Schnabel (1994) there are several other explanations for this phenomenon and one should not conclude that actual wages above contract wages are necessarily the result of efficiency wages.

In figure 5.4 the grey shaded area represents the average actual wage immediately after the wage negotiation when there is no shock. As can be seen there is still an asymmetry in the model, because a positive shock (ew_t^+) will lead to an increase of the average actual wage that is larger than the decrease that would result from a negative shock (ew_t^-) of the same amount. The difference is represented by the two dark shaded triangles.[9] However, the problem is much smaller with diverse firms than in a model with identical firms or only one firm. Since this seems to be an appropriate framework for the German situation, the problem is neglected in the empirical setup.

[9] If, alternatively, the contract wage would not be the wage of the median voter but e.g. the wage of the member with the lowest efficiency wage, the problem would reduce to only the lower triangle. The assumption implicit in the figure that the shock is additive is not realistic and only for diagrammatic convenience.

6. A Model of Involuntary Unemployment

With the reassuring results of the previous chapter, the natural next step is to build a structural model of the German labour market using the bargaining model of chapter 4. For this purpose it is necessary to discuss the level at which the bargain actually takes place in Germany. This issue has been neglected so far and the discussion treated the wage bargain on the level of an individual firm. This is easily generalized to the case of an employers association bargaining with a trade union, which is modeled as one firm with a utility given by aggregate profits of the member firms. The utility of the trade union can be treated in the same way. However, at a certain level of aggregation the question arises whether some of the variables can still be treated as exogenous to the bargain. This is the case for the economy wide unemployment rate, which is generally modeled as an exogenous factor in the union utility. If the bargain is on the level of the economy, this would clearly not be appropriate. Since in Germany bargaining generally takes place on the industry level, I will concentrate on this case and take the unemployment rate as exogenous to the bargain. However, it will turn out that at least for the proportional solution, the aggregate model for the economy as a whole will not be affected by this decision.

In this chapter I discuss a real approach to wage bargaining. With real approach I want to emphasize the fact that it is the level of the real wage that is determined in the bargain. The theory therefore establishes a kind of real rigidity that can lead to involuntary unemployment in equilibrium. As such the model serves as substitute for the labour market in the classical macroeconomic model and tries to explain the long-run behaviour of real wages and employment, based on a model of wage bargaining. The firm utility is discussed first in section 6.1, followed by the union utility in section 6.2. In section 6.3 the two concepts are used to determine the bargaining solution. The bargaining solution with the given utilities leads to a plausible description of the long-run behaviour of wages and employment as shown in section 6.4. From this the structural equations of the econometric model are developed in section 6.5. Finally, the appendix in section 6.6 discusses the long-run equivalence of a dynamic version of the applied utility.

6.1 The Firm

In the trade union literature it is real pure economic profit that is generally used as firm utility U_f. The following analysis differs from this concept. As a general principle I assume that the capital stock is taken as given for the bargain and I will not consider the interaction of wage bargaining and investment as in Grout (1984) and Van der Ploeg (1987). Instead of real profits, I take the total real income of the factor capital π_r, i.e. pure economic profits plus capital costs divided by the producer price, as the utility of the firm. This concept fits better to a union utility that is something similar to the real wage sum. Whether this assumption is reasonable can hardly be decided by theory and seems to be mainly an empirical question. It suggests an interpretation of the bargain as a distributional conflict between labour and capital. Since the utility is stated as net utility, normalized to a fallback point of zero, this concept implicitly assumes that the firm is not able to put the capital stock to a different use in the same period and that the firm makes losses if no bargain is reached. This might be a strong assumption, but, at least for Germany, the concept of a fallback point is somehow problematic anyway, because the consequences of a failure in the negotiations at the level of an industry are difficult to evaluate. The assumption made here is mainly for convenience and the qualitative results are quite robust to changes in the specification of the fallback point.

Second, since the union in its utility takes account of social insurance contributions and wage taxes paid by the workers, it is reasonable to assume that in the firm utility the level of taxes, given by t_p, will be reflected at least partially. Therefore, I am a bit more general than using simply the level of real capital income and allow for taxes, leading to:

$$U_f = \pi_r(1 - t_p)^v , \tag{6.1}$$

where the polar cases of gross real capital income and net real capital income are represented by values of $v = 0$ and $v = 1$ respectively.[1]

In a competitive environment, the following variables will determine nominal capital income π_c of the firm

$$\pi_c = \pi_c(\tau, w_g, p_m, p, K) , \tag{6.2}$$

[1] Of course this is only a crude approximation of the real tax scheme. As at other points in the derivation of the model there is a trade-off between preserving loglinearity on the one hand and generality on the other hand. The approach of this book is to keep the model loglinear. Clearly this strategy necessitates several quite restrictive assumptions. But it seems to be superior to a strategy where the model is kept as general as possible and in the empirical analysis a loglinear approximation is used. The loglinear approximation does not make explicit whether such a functional form could be theoretically admissible for a certain technology and preference structure or not. Even if the loglinear form is admissible, one often loses information, because at least some of the parameter restrictions that are implied by the theory are not clear from the approximation.

where τ is the state of technology, w_g is hourly labour costs to the firm, p_m is the price for materials, p is the price for output and K is the capital stock. From this the labour demand function can be derived, given by

$$L = L(\tau, w_g, p_m, p, K) . \tag{6.3}$$

In the following analysis a Cobb-Douglas production function is used

$$Y = \tau L^{\alpha} K^{\beta} M^{\gamma} , \tag{6.4}$$

where M denotes materials. Under the assumption of perfect competition and decreasing returns to scale this leads to the following capital income function

$$\begin{aligned} \pi_c = {} & A p^{\frac{1}{1-(\alpha+\gamma)}} w_g^{-\frac{\alpha}{1-(\alpha+\gamma)}} p_m^{-\frac{\gamma}{1-(\alpha+\gamma)}} \\ & K^{\frac{\beta}{1-(\alpha+\gamma)}} \tau^{\frac{1}{1-(\alpha+\gamma)}} , \end{aligned} \tag{6.5}$$

where A is some constant that depends on α and γ. The corresponding labour demand function is then

$$\begin{aligned} L = {} & \hat{A} p^{\frac{1}{1-(\alpha+\gamma)}} w_g^{-\frac{\alpha}{1-(\alpha+\gamma)}-1} \\ & p_m^{-\frac{\gamma}{1-(\alpha+\gamma)}} K^{\frac{\beta}{1-(\alpha+\gamma)}} \tau^{\frac{1}{1-(\alpha+\gamma)}} , \end{aligned} \tag{6.6}$$

where $\hat{A}$ is a constant. As is well known from microeconomic theory the profit function is homogeneous of degree one in all prices, while the labour demand function is homogeneous of degree zero in all prices. Therefore we can define real capital income as

$$\begin{aligned} \pi_r = {} & A \left(\frac{w_g}{p}\right)^{-\frac{\alpha}{1-(\alpha+\gamma)}} \left(\frac{p_m}{p}\right)^{-\frac{\gamma}{1-(\alpha+\gamma)}} \\ & K^{\frac{\beta}{1-(\alpha+\gamma)}} \tau^{\frac{1}{1-(\alpha+\gamma)}} \end{aligned} \tag{6.7}$$

and write the labour demand function as

$$\begin{aligned} L = {} & \hat{A} \left(\frac{w_g}{p}\right)^{-\frac{\alpha}{1-(\alpha+\gamma)}-1} \\ & \left(\frac{p_m}{p}\right)^{-\frac{\gamma}{1-(\alpha+\gamma)}} K^{\frac{\beta}{1-(\alpha+\gamma)}} \tau^{\frac{1}{1-(\alpha+\gamma)}} . \end{aligned} \tag{6.8}$$

For the discussion in the following paragraph it will be convenient to employ a short notation

$$\pi_r = A \left(\frac{w_g}{p}\right)^{s} \hat{z} \tag{6.9}$$

$$L = \hat{A} \left(\frac{w_g}{p}\right)^{s-1} \hat{z} \tag{6.10}$$

to facilitate the exposition.

In a non-competitive environment demand Y takes the role of the output price, leading to

$$\pi_r = \pi_r(\tau, w_g, p_m, K, Y) \quad (6.11)$$
$$L = L(\tau, w_g, p_m, K, Y) \;, \quad (6.12)$$

which is the more general specification. However, under the assumption of an isoelastic demand function of the form

$$Y = \kappa p^{-\delta} \qquad \kappa > 0 \quad (6.13)$$
$$-\frac{\partial Y}{\partial p}\frac{p}{Y} = \delta > 1 \quad (6.14)$$

the real capital income and labour demand functions have the same form as in the competitive case. The constants A and $\hat{A}$ contain the demand elasticity and the output price will be endogenous, of course. Therefore the results of the following analysis extend to this case as well.

6.2 The Union

While the utility of the firm, whether given by firm profit or capital income, is a standard concept in microeconomic theory, the notion of a utility function of a trade union is much less straightforward. In the literature one can find a large number of possible candidates. An early suggestion by Dunlop (1950) was wage bill maximization:

$$U_i = w_i L_i \;. \quad (6.15)$$

In contrast to the previous discussion I discriminate here between aggregate and industry variables that are indicated by a subscript i. The wage bill utility can be seen as special case of a general Cobb-Douglas utility function of the form

$$U_i = w_i^a L_i^b \quad a, b > 0 \;. \quad (6.16)$$

Generally, the relevant wage concept for this utility is the real after tax consumption wage. This differs from real hourly labour costs and it is convenient to split this difference in two parts.

The difference between the producer price p_i and the consumption price p_c is the so-called price wedge

$$pw_i = \frac{p_i}{p_c} \;. \quad (6.17)$$

The difference between labour costs w_{ig} and the net wage $\bar{w}_{in}$ is the so-called tax wedge

$$tw = \frac{w_{ig}}{\bar{w}_{in}} , \tag{6.18}$$

which is assumed to be the same in all sectors. Using these definitions the utility can be written as

$$\begin{aligned} U_i &= \left(\frac{\bar{w}_{in}}{p_c}\right)^a L_i^b \\ &= \left(\frac{w_{ig}}{p_i}\right)^a L_i^b \left(\frac{pw_i}{tw}\right)^a . \end{aligned} \tag{6.19}$$

This specification assumes that the price wedge and the tax wedge enter union utility symmetrically. However, this is possibly not the case. The members of the union will receive at least part of the social insurance contributions in the form of non-wage entitlements. Therefore, it is reasonable to assume that the influence of the tax wedge might be lower than the influence of the price wedge, which can be expressed by a different power of the tax wedge in the union utility

$$\begin{aligned} U_i &= \left(\frac{w_{in}}{p_c}\right)^a L_i^b \\ &= \left(\frac{w_{ig}}{p_i}\right)^a L_i^b pw_i{}^a tw^{-f} , \end{aligned} \tag{6.20}$$

where $0 < f < a$ and w_{in} is the wage that is relevant for the union.

This utility is extremely simple, but like the Cobb-Douglas production function it will be necessary to assume a utility of this form if the loglinear structure of the model is to be preserved. Though, it will be possible to allow for a bit more general specification as will be shown later.

If one combines this definition of union utility with the labour demand function of the firm derived above, the utility can be written as:

$$U_i = \left(\frac{w_{ig}}{p_i}\right)^a \left(\hat{A}\left(\frac{w_{ig}}{p_i}\right)^{s-1} \hat{z}\right)^b pw_i{}^a tw^{-f} . \tag{6.21}$$

For simplicity it is assumed that the bargain is over labour costs. If the tax wedge is exogenous it is in fact irrelevant which of the wage variables is bargained over. For a bargaining problem to exist it is necessary that the union utility increases with the wage. The condition for this is

$$a + (s-1)b > 0 , \tag{6.22}$$

which says that the union has to value wages sufficiently high or labour sufficiently low to assure that a higher wage increases utility.[2]

Of course this specification of utility is not very reasonable in many circumstances, because alternatives that are available in the economy do not play a role in the utility. I do not intend to give a survey of all specifications that have been suggested (see e.g. Oswald, 1985). For the present framework a quite general functional form, suggested by Manning (1993), will be convenient. In order to arrive at a loglinear model, a simplified version will be applied. Since this utility includes intertemporal considerations it will be necessary to introduce time t as additional subscript. The utility is given by

$$U_{it} = (V_{it} - \hat{V}_t) L_{it}^b , \tag{6.23}$$

where V_{it} is the value of employment in the sector and $\hat{V}_t$ is the value of alternatives that are available to the workers elsewhere. The value functions are defined as

$$V_{it} = \frac{w_{int}}{p_{ct}} + \delta_t (q_{t+1} V_{t+1}^u + (1 - q_{t+1}) V_{t+1}) , \tag{6.24}$$

where δ_t is the discount factor and q_{t+1} is the probability of a worker who is employed in this period being unemployed in the next period. The value of being unemployed in the next period is denoted by V_{t+1}^u and the value of being employed in the next period by V_{t+1}. The definition of the value of being unemployed is given by

$$V_t^u = \frac{r_t}{p_{ct}} + \delta_t (\bar{q}_{t+1} V_{t+1}^u + (1 - \bar{q}_{t+1}) V_{t+1}) , \tag{6.25}$$

where r_t is unemployment benefits and $\bar{q}_{t+1}$ is the probability of a worker who is unemployed in this period being unemployed in the next period. The value of alternatives in the economy is given by

$$\hat{V}_t = \eta_t V_t + (1 - \eta_t) V_t^u , \tag{6.26}$$

where η_t is the probability of finding another job at date t.

6.3 The Bargaining Solution

First, I derive the solution for the case of a simple Cobb-Douglas utility and then go on to the more general specification of Manning. To save notation,

[2] If this condition is satisfied, the union utility will be monotonically increasing in the wage. This might seem a bit strange, since it implies that a monopoly union with such a utility function will set the wage as high as possible. However, in a bargaining framework it is necessary that the union prefers higher wages at least in a neighborhood of the bargaining solution. Therefore, one can think of this utility as an approximation to an arbitrary utility in this range.

a symmetry condition is imposed from the beginning. If all sectors are the same the proportional solution is given for all sectors by

$$\frac{U}{\pi_r(1-t_p)^v} = \frac{\left(\frac{w_g}{p}\right)^a \left(\hat{A}\left(\frac{w_g}{p}\right)^{s-1} \hat{z}\right)^b pw^a tw^{-f}}{A\left(\frac{w_g}{p}\right)^s \hat{z}(1-t_p)^v} = c\,, \tag{6.27}$$

where c is a constant given by the weights of the solution. This can be solved for real labour costs as

$$\frac{w_g}{p} = \left(A\hat{A}^{-b}\hat{z}^{1-b}pw^{-a}tw^f c(1-t_p)^v\right)^{\frac{1}{a+(s-1)b-s}} \,. \tag{6.28}$$

From this it is easy to derive equilibrium employment through resubstitution of the bargained wage in the employment equation

$$L = \hat{A}\left(A\hat{A}^{-b}\hat{z}^{1-b}pw^{-a}tw^f c(1-t_p)^v\right)^{\frac{s-1}{a+(s-1)b-s}} \hat{z}\,. \tag{6.29}$$

In the same manner it is possible to derive equilibrium employment for the specification using the more general utility of Manning introduced above. The proportional solution in a symmetric equilibrium is given by:

$$\frac{U_t}{\pi_{rt}(1-t_{pt})^v} = \frac{(V_t-\hat{V}_t)L_t^b}{\pi_{rt}(1-t_{pt})^v} = c\,. \tag{6.30}$$

The definitions of the value functions imply

$$V_t - \hat{V}_t = (1-\eta_t)(V_t - V_t^u)\,. \tag{6.31}$$

The second term is defined as

$$V_t - V_t^u = \frac{w_{nt}}{p_{ct}} - \frac{r_t}{p_{ct}} + \delta_t(\bar{q}_{t+1} - q_{t+1})(V_{t+1} - V_{t+1}^u)\,. \tag{6.32}$$

In contrast to Manning I do not consider a dynamic version of this model and simplify things drastically by assuming that $\bar{q}_{t+1} = q_{t+1}$ for every t. This might seem a quite strong and not very realistic assumption, but not much additional insight for the long-run behaviour of wages can be gained from the dynamic model, building on the difference between these probabilities, as discussed in the appendix to this chapter.

A further simplification can be made by defining a replacement ratio ρ_t as

$$\frac{r_t}{p_{ct}} = \rho_t \frac{w_{nt}}{p_{ct}}\,. \tag{6.33}$$

Using both assumptions the proportional solution simplifies to

$$\frac{\left((1-\eta_t)(1-\rho_t)\frac{w_{nt}}{p_{ct}}\right)L_t^b}{\pi_{rt}(1-t_{pt})^v} = c\,. \tag{6.34}$$

As can be seen, in the *aggregate*, i.e. in the symmetric equilibrium, this is a simple modification of the solution in the Cobb-Douglas case. There are two additional factors the wage is discounted with. For the empirical analysis it is necessary to proxy for η_t. This is the channel through which the aggregate unemployment or employment rate comes in. In the present model it turns out that the employment rate

$$e_t = \frac{L_t}{N_t} \tag{6.35}$$

will be more convenient, where N_t represents labour supply per sector. The approximation used is then

$$(1-\eta_t) = h e_t^{-d}\,, \tag{6.36}$$

where $h, d > 0$. Of course, the unemployment rate is a more straightforward proxy for $(1-\eta_t)$, the probability not to find a job elsewhere in the economy. But using the unemployment rate here would destroy the loglinear structure of the model at this stage and necessitate a linear approximation later. This leads to

$$\frac{\left((1-\rho_t)hN_t^d\frac{w_{nt}}{p_{ct}}\right)L_t^{b-d}}{\pi_{rt}(1-t_{pt})^v} = c\,. \tag{6.37}$$

The derivation of the equilibrium wage and employment equations is equivalent to the Cobb-Douglas case:

$$\frac{w_{gt}}{p_t} = \left(A\hat{A}^{-(b-d)}\hat{z}_t^{1-(b-d)}pw_t^{-1}tw_t^f(1-t_{pt})^v(1-\rho_t)^{-1}h^{-1}N_t^{-d}c\right)^{\frac{1}{1+(s-1)(b-d)-s}} \tag{6.38}$$

$$L_t = \left(A\hat{A}^{-(b-d)}\hat{z}_t^{1-(b-d)}pw_t^{-1}tw_t^f(1-t_{pt})^v(1-\rho_t)^{-1}h^{-1}N_t^{-d}c\right)^{\frac{s-1}{1+(s-1)(b-d)-s}} \cdot\hat{A}\hat{z}_t\,. \tag{6.39}$$

The employment equation can easily be transformed into an equation determining the employment rate by dividing by N_t on both sides

$$e_t = \hat{A}\left(A\hat{A}^{-(b-d)}\hat{z}_t^{1-(b-d)}pw^{-1}tw^f(1-t_{pt})^v(1-\rho_t)^{-1}h^{-1}c\right)^{\frac{s-1}{1+(s-1)(b-d)-s}} \cdot\hat{z}_tN_t^{\frac{-d(s-1)}{1+(s-1)(b-d)-s}-1}\,. \tag{6.40}$$

The next section shows that this equation delivers a reasonable long-run model for the employment rate.

6.4 Bargaining as a Theory of the Long Run

For the model of the last section to be a plausible description of the evolution of wages and employment over time, it seems necessary to impose the restriction that $\hat{z}_t$, the so-called productivity variables (Manning, 1993), do not influence equilibrium employment. If $\hat{z}_t$ had an influence, this would lead to the implausible result that the employment rate depends on the state of technology or the capital stock. Since these variables increase permanently over time, the employment rate would either decrease or increase permanently. This is not the case, however.[3]

As can be seen from equation (6.29) this condition implies in the case of a Cobb-Douglas utility of the union

$$\frac{(1-b)(s-1)}{a+(s-1)b-s}+1=0 \Leftrightarrow a=1\,. \tag{6.41}$$

With the more general utility introduced in equation (6.23) this condition was implicitly imposed from the beginning, because the difference between the two value functions enters the utility with a power of one. The Cobb-Douglas case is under this assumption only a restricted version of this utility and will not play a further role in the discussion. The productivity variables $\hat{z}$ therefore drop out of equation (6.40) which simplifies to

$$e_t = \hat{A}\left(A\hat{A}^{-(b-d)}pw^{-1}tw^{f}(1-t_{pt})^{v}(1-\rho_t)^{-1}h^{-1}c\right)^{\frac{s-1}{1+(s-1)(b-d)-s}} N_t^{\frac{-d(s-1)}{1+(s-1)(b-d)-s}-1}\,. \tag{6.42}$$

From this equation the determinants of employment are easily identified. Employment is determined by labour supply, the capital income tax, the price and tax wedge and the replacement ratio. All other factors are constants. Of course the parameter c offers a nice possibility to consider several political pressure variables in an ad hoc way, but, as will be shown, this is not necessary to explain the rise in German unemployment.[4]

[3] The empirical analysis in chapter 7 uses data over a time span of thirty-three years. Of course, one could argue that this is not long enough to exclude influences of technology or the capital stock a priori. Therefore, I return to the empirical support for this practice at several points in the discussion.

[4] An implication of the exclusion of the productivity variables is that the price of materials does not affect the employment rate. This might seem a strange feature in light of the strong rise in unemployment in many industrialized countries after the oil price shocks. But one has to keep in mind that the model presented above

The reduced employment rate equation does not depend on the productivity variables under certain parameter restrictions because the real wage *does* depend on these variables. As already noted in chapter 4, the Nash solution often leads to the opposite result, that wages do not react to changes in productivity. This has been of interest to macroeconomists because it can explain the lack of cyclical movements in the real wage that has first been discovered by Dunlop (1938) and Tarshis (1939). Since then the topic has been further analyzed in several papers (Neftci, 1978; Geary and Kennan, 1982; Bils, 1985; Garman and Richards, 1992; Mocan and Kudret, 1993; Solon et al., 1994, among others) with conflicting results. Some studies find procyclical, some countercyclical real wages and some do not find any consistent pattern.[5]

However, if the real wage is indeed not cyclical it is still not clear whether this model can serve as an explanation. As noted by Blanchard and Summers (1986), this feature is not very realistic in the long-run. They say that "to rescue this line of thought, it must be argued that real wages are rigid along some 'norm', which may increase over time" (p. 26). For a theory of the long-run it is exactly this norm that has to be explained. However, as shown above, the trade union model with the proportional solution behaves quite differently and can serve as an explanation of the long-run behaviour of wages. A major drawback of course is that the model cannot explain both features at the same time. Further research in this direction is clearly necessary.

6.5 The Econometric Model

Since the model laid out in the previous section is loglinear in structure, the implied linear relation is easily derived by taking natural logarithms. If the variables in the model are best described as integrated processes, which is indeed the case in Germany, as shown in the next chapter, the long-run relation should state a cointegration vector for the series involved.

---

does not intend to describe cyclical phenomena and concentrates on the long-run determinants of employment. In the bargaining model it seems quite natural that the different variables influencing firm profit and labour demand enter the solution symmetrically. One might justify an asymmetric treatment by a different technology, but I find this not very convincing.

[5] A quite interesting piece of work has been done by Sumner and Silver (1989) for the US. They show that the results of earlier studies depend crucially on the sample period. Since demand and supply shocks should lead to different reactions of real wages it is not surprising that studies over long time horizons have difficulties to find a stable pro- or countercyclical relationship, because the shocks in the sample periods have different sources. If the sample is split in periods where demand shocks prevail and periods in which supply shocks prevail, a pattern of real wage cyclicality emerges which is consistent with standard Keynesian business cycle theory. Unfortunately, a similar study for Germany does not yet exist.

The equations for the structural relations can be written as

$$\ln \frac{w_{gt}}{p_t} = \ln c + f \ln tw_t + \ln \pi_{rt} + v \ln(1 - t_{pt}) - \ln pw_t - \ln h - \ln(1 - \rho_t) - d \ln N_t - (b - d) \ln L_t + \epsilon_{1t} \tag{6.43}$$

$$\ln L_t = \ln \hat{A} + (s - 1) \ln \frac{w_{gt}}{p_t} + \ln \hat{z}_t + \epsilon_{2t} , \tag{6.44}$$

where $\epsilon_{1t}, \epsilon_{2t}$ are stationary processes. While the second equation is a standard labour demand function, the first relation seems to be quite interesting. It offers the prospect of estimating the structural parameters of the union utility function. Unfortunately, a cointegration analysis of equation (6.43) even without the parameter restrictions was not successful. I do not conclude, however, from the failure to reject the null hypothesis of no cointegration, that the regression is spurious. I think it is the fundamentally different behaviour of wage income and capital income over the business cycle that makes the residual highly autoregressive and causes this result. As noted above, wages are not as flexible over the business cycle as the model used in this study suggests. Capital income in contrast is highly cyclical. This different short-run behaviour blurs any possible long-run relation in the observed time span from 1960 to 1993. Therefore I will not engage in estimating the parameters of this equation. Such an approach would only lead to poor estimates and would not contribute much to the question whether the theory developed so far is supported by empirical evidence. Instead I concentrate on the reduced form of the model in the further analysis, which is not as informative as a structural form, but still allows inference on several elasticities that are crucial for discriminating between different models as well as for policy analysis. Fortunately, the business cycle problem is less pronounced for this equation.

The following reduced form relations in loglinear form can be deduced

$$\ln \frac{w_{gt}}{p_t} = \delta_{10} + \delta_{11} \ln pw_t + \delta_{12} \ln tw_t + \delta_{11} \ln(1 - \rho_t) + \delta_{11} \ln c + \delta_{13} \ln N_t + \delta_{14} \ln \hat{z}_t + \delta_{15} \ln(1 - t_{pt}) + \epsilon_{3t} \tag{6.45}$$

$$\ln e_t = \delta_{20} + \delta_{21} \ln pw_t + \delta_{22} \ln tw_t + \delta_{21} \ln(1 - \rho_t) + \delta_{23} \ln N_t + \delta_{24} \ln(1 - t_{pt}) + \epsilon_{4t} , \tag{6.46}$$

where the δ_{ij} are functions of the structural parameters and $\epsilon_{3t}, \epsilon_{4t}$ are stationary processes. What is of importance for the empirical analysis are the following relations

$$v = -\frac{\delta_{24}}{\delta_{21}} \tag{6.47}$$

$$f = -\frac{\delta_{22}}{\delta_{21}} . \tag{6.48}$$

They allow the calculation of at least two important parameters of the structural model from the parameters of the second equation. A main advantage of the second equation is the exclusion of any productivity terms. It is not necessary to measure $\hat{z}_t$, a crucial point being the state of technology τ. Generally in empirical work τ is proxied by a linear time trend. However, as is indicated by empirical studies (Flaig and Steiner, 1993) technological progress in Germany is better described by a random walk. This result has to be taken with caution of course, since estimation of the state of technology is only possible under quite restrictive assumptions, as in the case of Solow residuals, or by estimation of the parameters of an underlying technology using the mentioned proxy variable in a first stage as in the study of Flaig and Steiner. But nonetheless this can be seen as an indication that the usual practice may not be appropriate in a cointegration analysis. I therefore decided to concentrate on the reduced form employment rate relation in the empirical analysis presented in the next chapter.

6.6 Appendix

This appendix discusses the properties of the model with a dynamic specification of the union utility. As will be shown, the steady state of the dynamic model differs from the equilibrium of the static model only by a factor depending on δ_t and $\bar{q}_{t+1} - q_{t+1}$ which are quite likely to be stationary variables or, in the deterministic model, can be assumed constant. Further, for reasonable values of b the steady state is the only non-explosive equilibrium.

The two equations that essentially determine the evolution of wages in the symmetric equilibrium are[6]:

$$\frac{(1-\eta_t)(V_t - V_t^u)L_t^b}{\pi_{rt}(1-t_{pt})^v} = c \tag{6.49}$$

$$V_t - V_t^u = \frac{w_{gt}}{p_t}\frac{pw_t}{tw_t^f}(1-\rho_t) + \delta_t(\bar{q}_{t+1} - q_{t+1})(V_{t+1} - V_{t+1}^u) \,. \tag{6.50}$$

To determine the properties of the system I assume that all variables except the wage are constant and employ the following short notation:

$$\hat{w}_t = k\bar{V}_t^\theta \tag{6.51}$$

$$\bar{V}_t = \hat{w}_t + \hat{\delta}\bar{V}_{t+1} \,, \tag{6.52}$$

[6] If the proxy for η is introduced before doing the stability analysis, the difference would be that one has to replace b by $b-d$ and $(1-\eta)$ by hN^{-d} in all equations.

where

$$\hat{w}_t = \frac{w_{gt}}{p}\frac{pw}{tw^f}(1-\rho) \tag{6.53}$$

$$k = \left(\frac{(1-\eta)(\hat{A}\hat{z})^b}{cA\hat{z}(1-t_p)^v}\right)^{-\frac{1}{b(s-1)-s}} \frac{pw}{tw^f}(1-\rho) \tag{6.54}$$

$$\theta = -\frac{1}{b(s-1)-s} \tag{6.55}$$

$$\bar{V}_t = V_t - V_t^u \tag{6.56}$$

$$\hat{\delta} = \delta(\bar{q}-q)\,. \tag{6.57}$$

The equilibrium under the assumption made in the main part $\hat{\delta} = 0$ is given by

$$\hat{w}^* = k^{\frac{1}{1-\theta}}\,, \tag{6.58}$$

as can be verified from equations (6.51) and (6.52) above.

Proposition 6.1
The steady state of the dynamic model is given by

$$\bar{w} = k^{\frac{1}{1-\theta}}(1-\hat{\delta})^{\frac{-\theta}{1-\theta}} = \hat{w}^*(1-\hat{\delta})^{\frac{-\theta}{1-\theta}}\,. \tag{6.59}$$

Proof: From the definitions the following relations can be derived:

$$\hat{w}_t = k\left(\hat{w}_t + \hat{\delta}\bar{V}_{t+1}\right)^\theta \tag{6.60}$$

$$\hat{w}_{t+1} = k\bar{V}_{t+1}^\theta\,. \tag{6.61}$$

Solving the second equation for V_{t+1} and substituting in the first equation gives a nonlinear first order difference equation for $\hat{w}_t$:

$$\hat{w}_t = k\left(\hat{w}_t + \hat{\delta}\left(\frac{1}{k}\hat{w}_{t+1}\right)^{\frac{1}{\theta}}\right)^\theta\,. \tag{6.62}$$

The stated result can be verified by setting $\hat{w}_t = \hat{w}_{t+1} = \bar{w}$ and solving for $\bar{w}$. ■

The steady state is only defined for $\theta \neq 1 \Leftrightarrow b \neq 1$ and only for these values stability is an issue.

Proposition 6.2
The dynamic model is asymptotically locally stable for

$$\frac{s - \frac{1-\hat{\delta}}{1+\hat{\delta}}}{s-1} < b < 1\,. \tag{6.63}$$

Proof: To determine the asymptotic properties of the model it is necessary to evaluate the first derivative of $\hat{w}_{t+1}$ with respect to $\hat{w}_t$ of the nonlinear equation at the steady state. Solving the model for $\hat{w}_{t+1}$ gives:

$$\hat{w}_{t+1} = \hat{\delta}^{-\theta} \left(\hat{w}_t^{\frac{1}{\theta}} - k^{\frac{1}{\theta}} \hat{w}_t \right)^{\theta} . \tag{6.64}$$

The first derivative is given by:

$$\frac{\partial \hat{w}_{t+1}}{\partial \hat{w}_t} = \hat{\delta}^{-\theta} \theta \left(\hat{w}_t^{\frac{1}{\theta}} - k^{\frac{1}{\theta}} \hat{w}_t \right)^{\theta - 1} \left(\frac{1}{\theta} \hat{w}_t^{\frac{1}{\theta} - 1} - k^{\frac{1}{\theta}} \right) . \tag{6.65}$$

Evaluating this at the steady state and rearranging leads to:

$$\left. \frac{\partial \hat{w}_{t+1}}{\partial \hat{w}_t} \right|_{\overline{w}} = \frac{1 - \theta(1 - \hat{\delta})}{\hat{\delta}} . \tag{6.66}$$

Stability of the nonlinear model requires the derivative at the steady state to be absolutely smaller than one. Assuming that $\hat{\delta} > 0$, which is equivalent to the plausible case $\bar{q} > q$, this is equal to:

$$-1 < \left. \frac{\partial \hat{w}_{t+1}}{\partial \hat{w}_t} \right|_{\overline{w}} < 1 \Leftrightarrow \frac{1 + \hat{\delta}}{1 - \hat{\delta}} > \theta > 1 . \tag{6.67}$$

From the definition of θ in equation (6.55) we know that

$$\theta = -\frac{1}{b(s-1) - s} > 1 \Leftrightarrow b < 1 \tag{6.68}$$

if $b > s/(s-1)$. If $b < s/(s-1)$ then $\theta < 0$. Further

$$\frac{1 + \hat{\delta}}{1 - \hat{\delta}} > \theta \Leftrightarrow \frac{s - \frac{1 - \hat{\delta}}{1 + \hat{\delta}}}{s - 1} < b \tag{6.69}$$

if $b > s/(s-1)$ which completes the proof. ■

Clearly, since $\hat{\delta}$ is likely to be substantially smaller than one, the range of stable equilibria is small. From condition (6.22) we know that in the Cobb-Douglas case the derivative of union utility with respect to the wage is positive if (with $a = 1$)

$$1 + (s-1)b > 0 \Leftrightarrow b < \frac{-1}{s-1} . \tag{6.70}$$

Because $s = -1$ would be a typical value for a Cobb-Douglas technology it is very unlikely that both conditions are satisfied at the same time even if $\hat{\delta}$ is close to one.

I think it is possible to give a simple intuition for this behaviour. Assume that $b < s/(s-1)$ and therefore $\theta < 0$. These are reasonable values and amount to the assumption that lower wages would require a higher net value $\bar{V}_t$ according to equation (6.51). However, lower wages have a negative impact on this net value, because of equation (6.52). As a result, to restore equilibrium, the net value in the next period has to be very high which requires even lower wages. If these explosive branches are excluded, the single remaining equilibrium path is the steady state equilibrium.

7. A Macroeconometric Analysis

With the theory developed in the previous chapter it is now possible to investigate whether the stated long-run relation is supported by data on the West German economy. The next section describes the data used in the study, which are simple aggregates from the national accounts and as such publicly available. The seasonal properties of the data are discussed in section 7.2, concentrating on the question of whether there are seasonal unit roots in the series and if so at which frequencies. A proper treatment of seasonality is important since cointegration tests can be quite sensitive to adjustment procedures. Having identified the correct seasonal filters, the cointegration analysis is carried out in section 7.3. In this section cointegration among the variables in the derived equation is checked and the cointegration vector is estimated with the fully modified procedure. The final section 7.4 concludes with a discussion of the results.

7.1 The Data

The first decision to be made is one of sample length. A study for reunited Germany using cointegration techniques is not possible yet, because the time span is still to short to reveal long term relations. For West Germany the available data is much better, reaching back to at least the sixties. I decided to use data on West Germany from 1960 to 1993. This sample covers substantially different periods in German economic history (see Giersch et al., 1992, for a survey) and stretches beyond German reunification. Stability is an important issue in this case and therefore an estimation technique is employed that allows to test for slow parameter changes as well as for sharp breaks in a cointegration framework.

A second choice concerns the frequency of the data used. As simulation studies have shown, increasing the time span and the frequency improves the power of unit root and cointegration tests, time span playing a more important role than frequency (Shiller and Perron, 1985; Lahiri and Nlandu, 1995). As quarterly data on all important variables are available for a time span that is equivalent to the available span of annual data, at least on an aggregate level, I therefore decided against annual data. As a consequence one has to think about an appropriate way to deal with the seasonality of the data, which makes the analysis more involved, but this additional effort seems justified.

The data used for the analysis are taken from different sources. For the estimation of equation (6.46) the following variables are used.

- The employment rate e_t is measured by the ratio of the employed and the workforce, defined by the sum of employed and unemployed. This is not the same as the official definition of the workforce which includes the self employed, but it seems to be appropriate with regard to the model.
- The price wedge pw_t is given by the ratio of GDP deflator and Consumer Price Index. Although the GDP deflator is not really appropriate, it is used here instead of the price index of total production which the Federal Statistical Office does not issue on a quarterly basis. The annual price index of total production, available from 1970 onwards, is very close to the GDP deflator and this substitution should therefore be a minor problem.
- The tax wedge tw_t is given by

$$tw_t = \frac{1 + socins_{1t}}{1 - wagetax_t - socins_{2t}}, \tag{7.1}$$

  where $socins_{1t}(socins_{2t})$ is defined as the ratio of the social insurance contributions of the employers (employees) and the gross sum of wages and $wagetax_t$ is defined as the ratio of the sum of wage taxes and the gross sum of wages.
- The statutory replacement ratio ρ_t has barely changed over the sample period and the available data from the Federal Labour Office that can be used to calculate the average replacement ratio seem to reflect the composition of the unemployed rather than changes in the rules. I have therefore not included a measure for the replacement ratio in the cointegration analysis. In any case, this variable cannot be an explanation for the trend in unemployment.
- The size of the workforce N_t is measured by the sum of the employed and unemployed times the average hours worked. This definition is a logical consequence of the definition of labour demand L_t. If labour demand is assumed to be demand for hours worked in the derivation of the equations above, then the size of the workforce has to be defined accordingly to lead to the correct employment rate.
- The tax on capital income t_{pt} is given by the ratio of taxes on income from wealth and entrepreneurship and the income from wealth and entrepreneurship itself. This variable conforms to the model only in a closed economy, because it is the average tax rate Germans pay on their income from entrepreneurship and wealth worldwide and this is not identical to the taxes paid on the capital income generated by firms operating in Germany. The assumption of a closed economy is possibly not innocuous in the case of Germany. However, there are two arguments that mitigate the problem. First, as argued in the introduction, the average tax rates on

capital income have gone down in Europe as a whole in the last twenty years. The plots of $(1 - t_{pt})$ below confirm that Germany's development was quite similar in this period. Therefore, the German average tax rate is a reasonable proxy for the European one, at least in the eighties and early nineties. Second, calculating the average tax rate for capital used by a firm is difficult, or even impossible. In bargaining at the level of an industry, the variable used in the econometric model here might well be the natural proxy for the taxation of capital income used by the bargaining parties themselves.

All data except the CPI are taken from the quarterly national accounts of the DIW, available on disk. The CPI is taken from the monthly reports of the German Bundesbank.

7.2 Seasonal Structure

In this section the seasonal properties of the data are analyzed. Before calculating test statistics, I provide a visual image of the seasonal characteristics of the data in the skip sample plots in figures 7.1, 7.2 and 7.3. As can be seen, maybe except for the employment rate, all the series display a visible trending behaviour in at least some of the quarters. In the given framework, this suggests the existence of seasonal unit roots in the autoregressive polynomial of the univariate representation of these series.

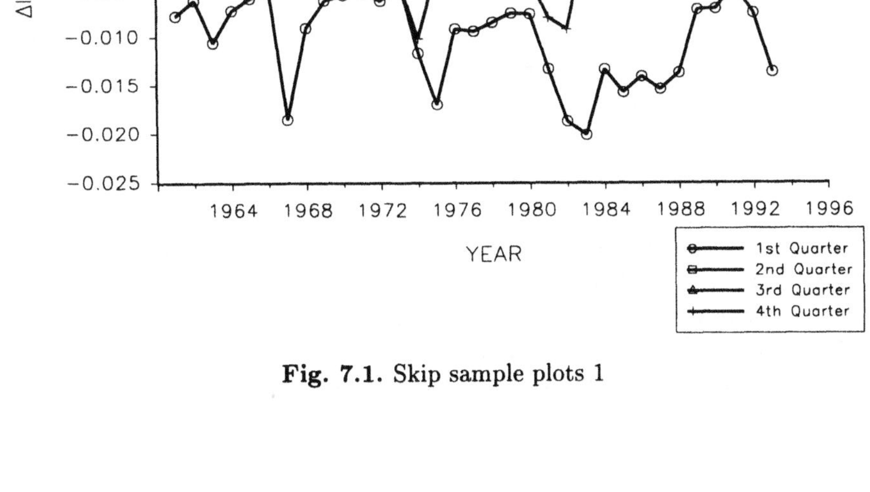

Fig. 7.1. Skip sample plots 1

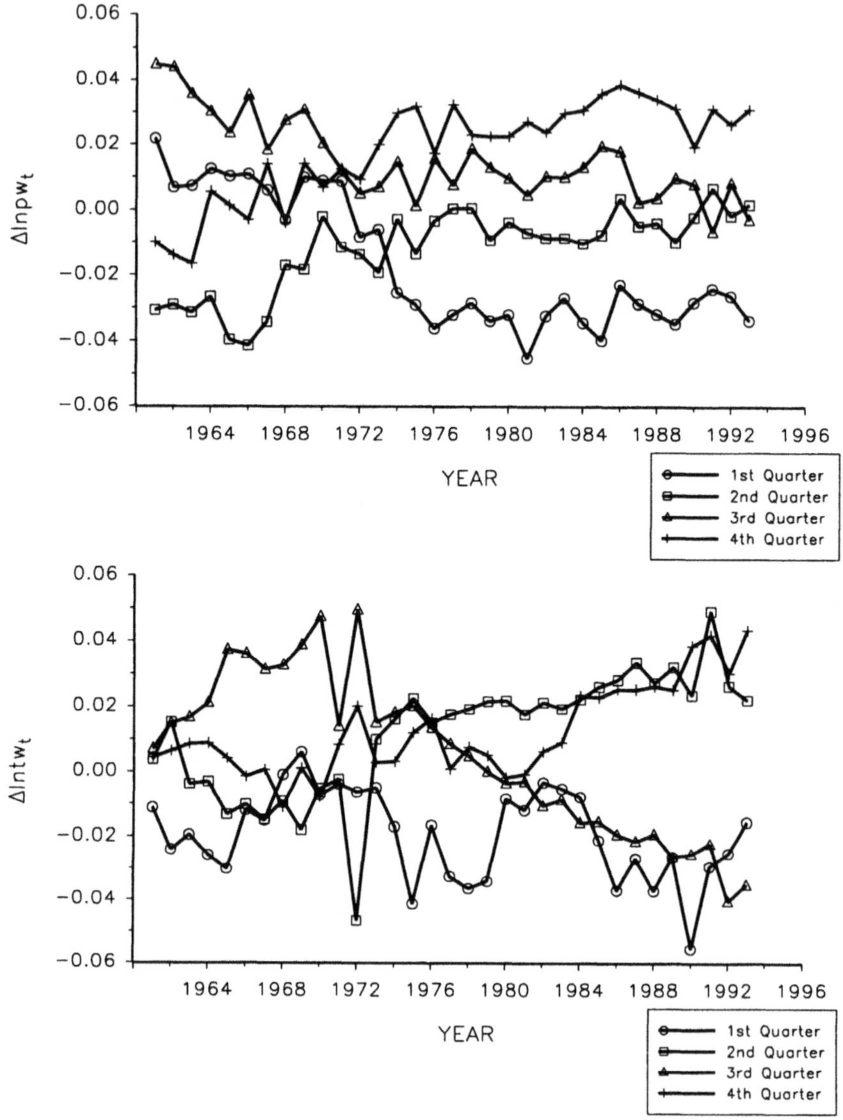

Fig. 7.2. Skip sample plots 2

Of course one cannot decide on behalf of such a plot at which seasonal frequencies these unit roots lie. A statistical criterion is therefore needed. For this purpose I calculate two test statistics as discussed in the methods chapter. The first is the HEGY test and the second is the CH test. For the CH test it is necessary to remove the unit root at the zero frequency before applying the test. For this to be a valid procedure, one should assure that there indeed is a unit root at this frequency, which is not known a priori. This problem is not

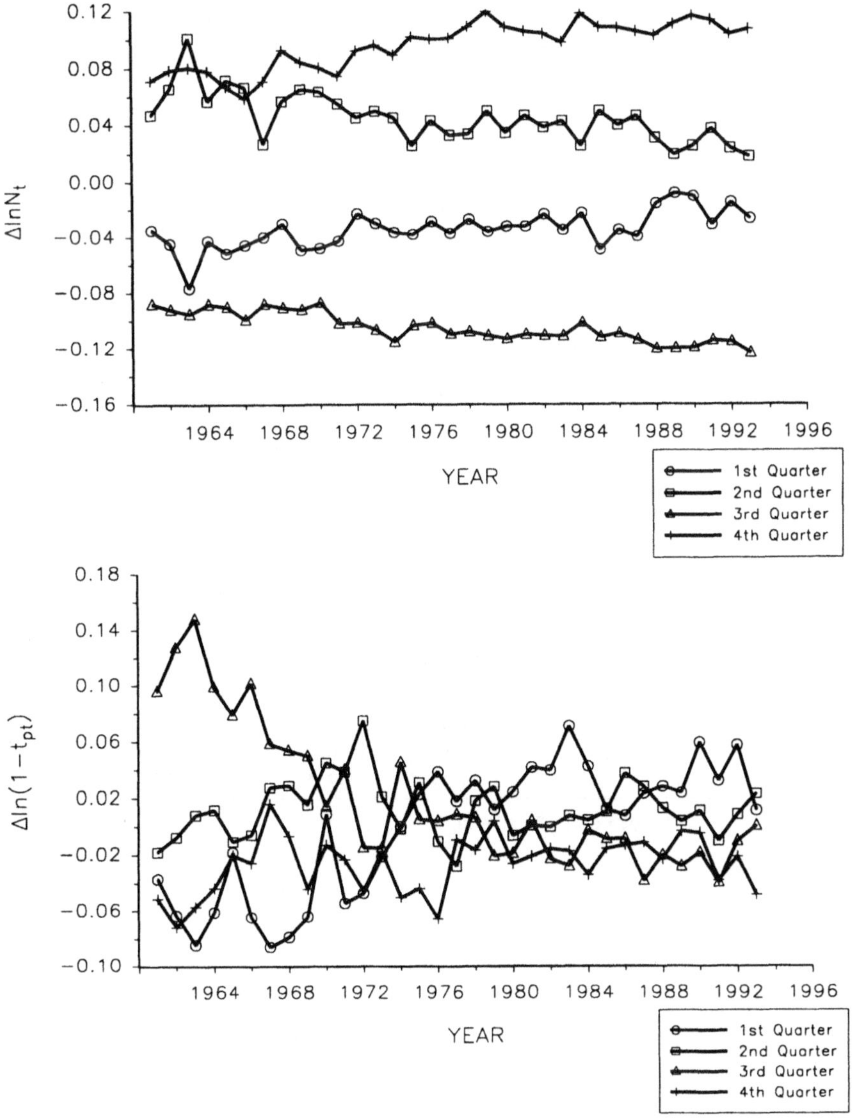

Fig. 7.3. Skip sample plots 3

encountered in case of the HEGY test, because hypothesis on both seasonal and nonseasonal unit roots can be tested in one framework. I therefore start with a HEGY test on the data in levels and then run a second one on the first differences. If the data have a single unit root on the nonseasonal frequency the first HEGY test should not reject this hypothesis while the second one should. The results in table (7.1) and table (7.2) indicate that this is indeed the case for all series under consideration. This result justifies the use of the first differences of the variables in the CH test below.

Table 7.1. HEGY tests I

	t-tests		F-test
	$\pi_1 = 0$	$\pi_2 = 0$	$\pi_3 = \pi_4 = 0$
$\ln e_t[2]$	-2.74	-2.06	7.38^{**}
$\ln pw_t[5]$	-2.35	-1.84	4.48
$\ln tw_t[5]$	-1.05	-0.19	2.63
$\ln N_t[3]$	-2.72	-5.48^{**}	2.65
$\ln(1-t_{pt})[7]$	-1.99	-3.44^{**}	2.29

* 10% sig., ** 5% sig.

Table 7.2. HEGY tests II

	t-tests		F-test
	$\pi_1 = 0$	$\pi_2 = 0$	$\pi_3 = \pi_4 = 0$
$\Delta \ln e_t[3]$	-3.89^{**}	-1.54	8.94^{**}
$\Delta \ln pw_t[7]$	-3.68^{**}	-2.28	3.53
$\Delta \ln tw_t[7]$	-3.03^{**}	-0.76	2.80
$\Delta \ln N_t[3]$	-5.14^{**}	-4.06^{**}	1.67
$\Delta \ln(1-t_{pt})[6]$	-5.02^{**}	-3.67^{**}	2.19

* 10% sig., ** 5% sig.

Table 7.3. CH tests

	unit-root tests	
	π	$\pi/2$
$\Delta \ln e_t$	0.73^{**}	0.39
$\Delta \ln pw_t$	9.28^{**}	0.35
$\Delta \ln tw_t$	6.92^{**}	1.43^{**}
$\Delta \ln N_t$	0.09	8.14^{**}
$\Delta \ln(1-t_{pt})$	0.23	5.16^{**}

* 10% sig., ** 5% sig.

The purpose of calculating two test statistics instead of one is to ensure that the results of the HEGY test are robust with regard to a change in the assumption about the DGP. That this might be necessary is suggested by the results in Hylleberg (1995). The crucial decision that has to be made when applying both tests is how to proceed when the tests give conflicting results. As a general principle I assume the existence of a unit root whenever there is no strong evidence against it, i.e. both tests indicate the absence of a unit root. The reason for this is my conjecture that a seasonal unit root in one of the series would cause more problems in the estimation of the cointegration vector than over differencing would do. As is shown in Engle et al. (1989) OLS estimation of the cointegration vector at the nonseasonal frequency can be inconsistent if a seasonal unit root is left in one of the series and there is also the problem of a spurious regression as discussed in Abeysinghe (1994). The problems with over differencing do not seem to be of comparable importance.

As can be seen from the tables, strong evidence against the existence of a seasonal unit root exists only for $\ln e_t$ at the annual frequency and for $\ln N_t$ and $\ln(1 - t_{pt})$ at the semiannual frequency. There is one conflicting result for $\ln pw_t$ at the annual frequency. In this case I decided, according to the conjecture made above, to assume the existence of a seasonal unit root at this frequency.

Since only the possibility of cointegration at the zero frequency is considered, it is necessary to adjust the series in an appropriate way, such that only this unit root is left in the series. The results therefore suggest that the correct filters are given by

- $0,5(1 + L)$ for $\ln e_t$
- $0,25(1 + L + L^2 + L^3)$ for $\ln pw_t, \ln tw_t$
- $0,5(1 + L^2)$ for $\ln N_t$ and $\ln(1 - t_{pt})$.

The filtered series were regressed on the trigonometric seasonal dummy of the frequency not removed by the filter what lead to the seasonally adjusted series, used in the following.

7.3 Cointegration Analysis

In this section I present the main results from the cointegration analysis[1] of equation (6.46). The univariate properties of the series have been established in the last section and it is possible to calculate the cointegration tests without further pretesting. The adjusted series used for this purpose are shown in figures 7.4 to 7.6.

For these series the model derived in chapter 6 suggests the following cointegration relation

$$\ln e_t = \bar{\delta}_{20} + \delta_{21} \ln pw_t + \delta_{22} \ln tw_t + \delta_{23} \ln N_t + \delta_{24} \ln(1 - t_{pt}) + \epsilon_t \,. \quad (7.2)$$

The next step in the analysis is to test for the number of cointegration vectors in the space spanned by the included variables. I have calculated three

[1] All cointegration tests and fully modified estimations have been calculated using the COINT2.0 GAUSS package of Ouliaris&Phillips.

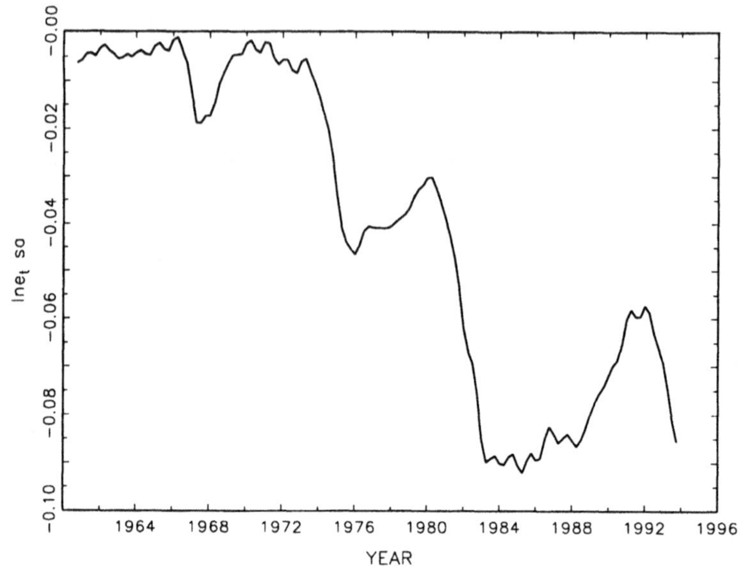

Fig. 7.4. Adjusted series 1

different cointegration tests. The results are given in table 7.4. According to a study by Haug (1996) the Stock and Watson (1988) statistic SW and the P_z statistic of Phillips and Ouliaris (1990) are performing best in terms of power when the regressors are endogenous, what is likely to be the case here. The trace statistic Joh developed in Johansen (1988) is also reported. It displayed only small size distortions in Haug's study. For the Johansen test the optimal lag length was determined by an AIC criterion using a VAR in levels. For the Phillips and Ouliaris test and the Stock and Watson test a Bartlett kernel and the bandwidth selection suggested by Andrews (1991), was used.

Table 7.4. Cointegration tests

	Joh	SW	P_z
$\ln e_t, \ln pw_t, \ln tw_t, \ln N_t, \ln(1-t_{pt})$	98.00**	−60.99**	172.36*

* 10% sig., ** 5% sig.

As can be seen from the table, the statistics clearly support the hypothesis of at least one cointegration vector. The trace statistic Joh and the common trends statistic SW for the hypothesis of no cointegration vector do both reject at the five percent level. The P_z statistic rejects this hypothesis at the ten percent level. As additional information it is useful to check whether there really is only one cointegration vector, which can be done within the Johansen

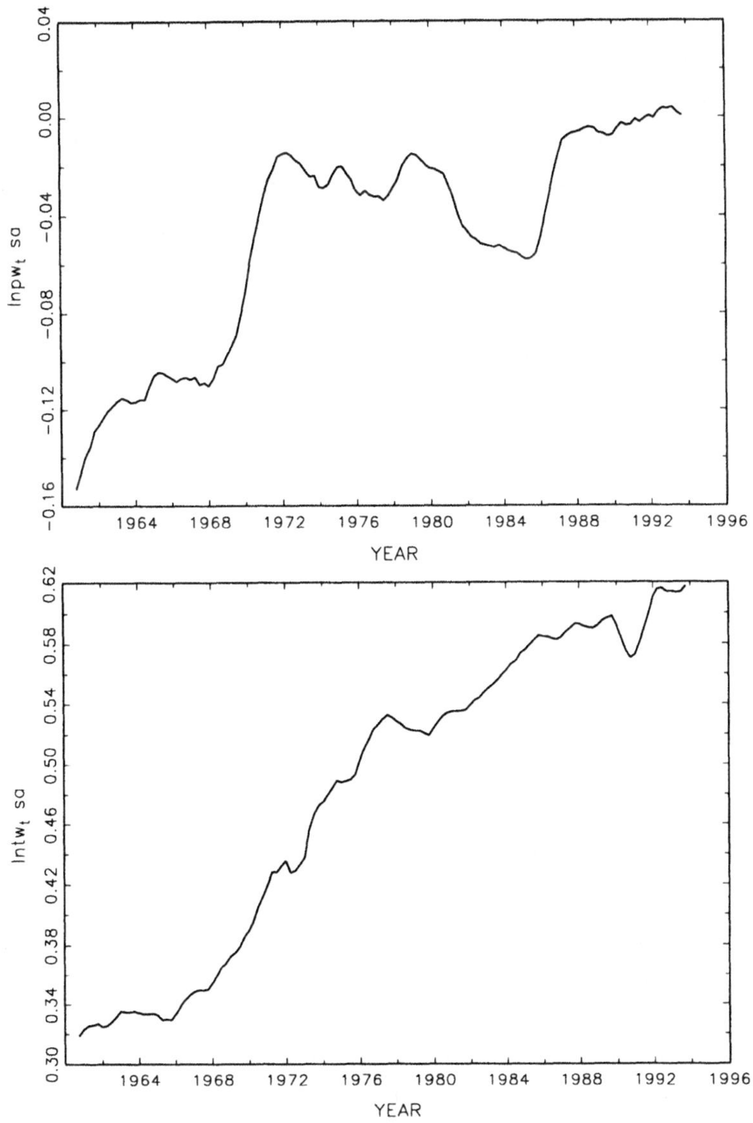

Fig. 7.5. Adjusted series 2

procedure. The trace statistic for the hypothesis of one cointegration vector gives a value of 35.5 far below the ten percent critical value and the hypothesis cannot be rejected. Therefore, it is justified to assume that there is only a single cointegration vector. This result supports the model and shows that the exclusion of other trending variables like technological progress is not rejected by the data.

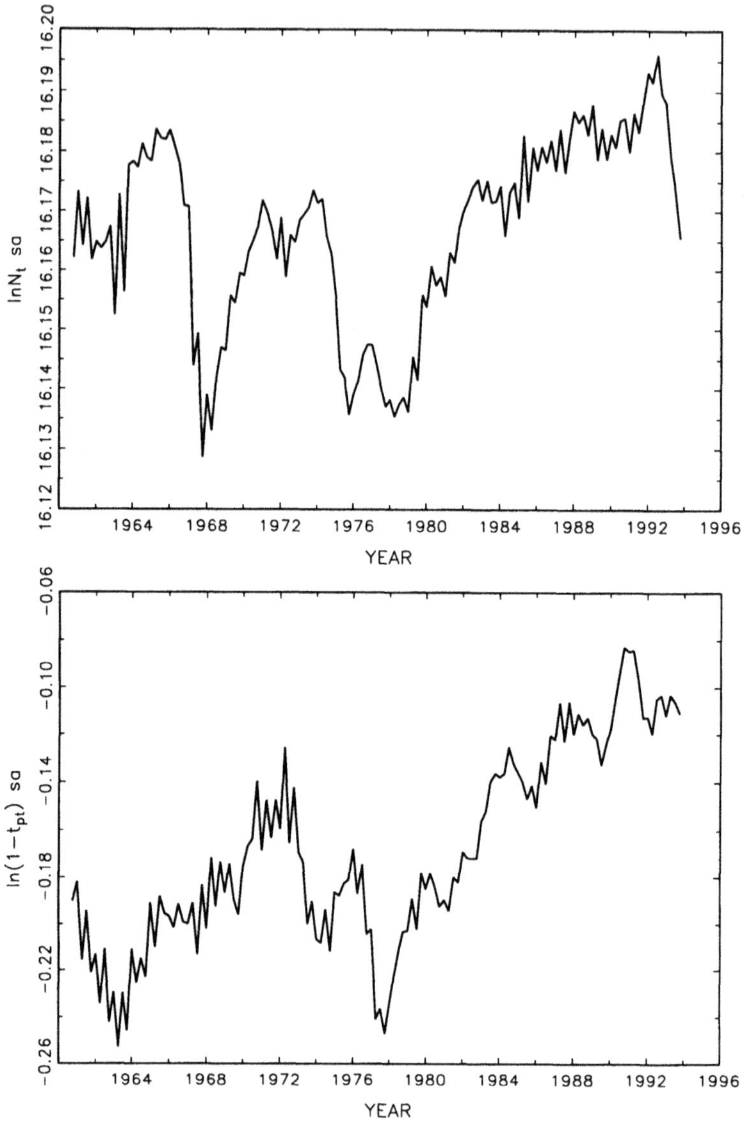

Fig. 7.6. Adjusted series 3

The next step is to estimate the parameters of the cointegration vector, which can be done consistently by OLS, as shown in chapter 2. However, as is also discussed in this chapter, one should expect that the fully modified procedure by Phillips and Hansen (1990) has efficiency gains and has the further advantage that in contrast to OLS this procedure leads to asymptotically χ^2 distributed Wald-statistics under quite general conditions. Nonetheless, it might be of interest to compare the results with the OLS estimate that is also reported. For the fully modified estimation I used again a Bartlett kernel and the bandwidth selection suggested by Andrews (1991).

The results of the estimation are given in table 7.5. The first thing to note is that the price wedge, the tax wedge and the capital income tax are significant in the FM-OLS estimation. The labour supply variable in contrast is not significant, what suggests the reestimation of the model with this variable excluded. This is reported in table 7.6. As can be seen, the constant that was not significant in the first estimation has now a significant positive parameter as predicted by the model. The other variables remain significant even at the one percent level. A plot of $\ln e_t$ together with the fitted values using the results of this estimation is given in figure 7.7.

Table 7.5. Estimation 1

	$\ln pw_t$	$\ln tw_t$	$\ln N_t$	$\ln(1-t_{pt})$	*constant*
OLS					
Coefficients	0.55	−0.45	0.07	−0.16	−0.96
t-statistics	17.52	−31.51	1.26	−5.82	−1.07
FM-OLS					
Coefficients	0.56	−0.45	0.06	−0.15	−0.72
t-statistics	9.14**	−16.61**	0.52	−2.70**	−0.41

* 10% sig., ** 5% sig.

Table 7.6. Estimation 2

	$\ln pw_t$	$\ln tw_t$	$\ln(1-t_{pt})$	*constant*
OLS				
Coefficients	0.54	−0.44	−0.14	0.18
t-statistics	17.69	−31.41	−6.19	17.86
FM-OLS				
Coefficients	0.54	−0.45	−0.13	0.18
t-statistics	9.43**	−17.10**	−3.03**	9.87**

* 10% sig., ** 5% sig.

The results imply the following estimates of the structural parameters

$$\hat{v} = -\frac{\hat{\delta}_{24}}{\hat{\delta}_{21}} = 0.24 \tag{7.3}$$

$$\hat{f} = -\frac{\hat{\delta}_{22}}{\hat{\delta}_{21}} = 0.83\,, \tag{7.4}$$

which are consistent with the theory in sign and magnitude. Both the parameter of the tax wedge and of the capital income tax, are positive and

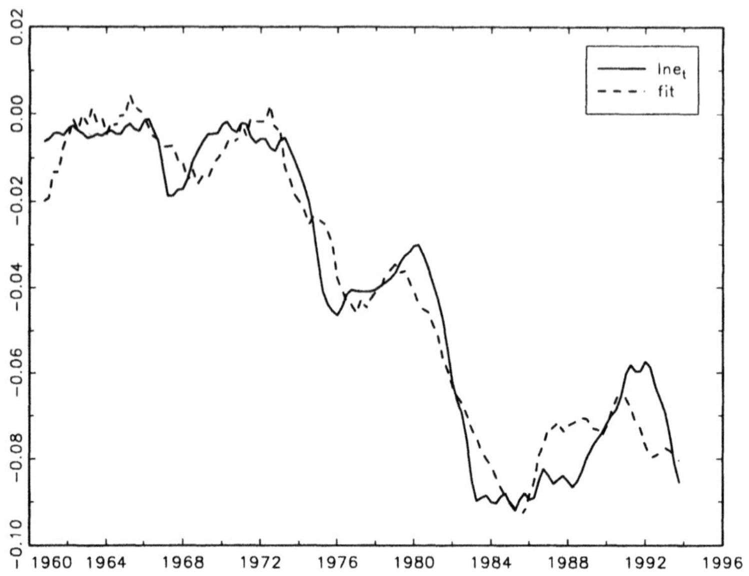

Fig. 7.7. Fitted values from estimation 2: FM-OLS

smaller than one. The results are further examined and discussed in the next section.[2]

Table 7.7. Hansen's stability tests

	SupF	*MeanF*	L_c
Statistic	13.67	7.38*	0.51

* 10% sig., ** 5% sig.

An important point in the analysis is the stability of the equation. The great advantage of the fully modified procedure for this analysis is that it allows for stability tests that detect slow changes as well as sharp breaks. These tests have been proposed by Hansen (1992). The results for the model without the labour supply variable are given in table 7.7. The region for the *SupF* and the *MeanF* statistic has been set to [0.15, 0.85] as in Hansen (1992). As can be seen, the *SupF* statistic that is appropriate for testing sharp structural breaks does not reject. And the other two statistics show only minor evidence for slowly changing parameters as well. Only the *MeanF* statistic

[2] Another possible test for the relevance of productivity terms in the equation would be the inclusion of these variables in the estimation at this stage. However, as noted above, the problems with the calculation of total factor productivity speak against such an approach.

rejects the null hypothesis at the ten percent level, while the L_c statistic does not reject at this level of significance. The last two statistics can also be interpreted as cointegration tests with the null hypothesis of cointegration. The process is therefore quite stable over a long historical period with remarkably different levels of unemployment. However, since there is some evidence from the $MeanF$ statistic that the parameters are not stable, one should clearly try to reestimate the model for Germany as a whole when the available time span is long enough.

7.4 Discussion

The first and most important thing to say about the results is that the model works. The model can serve as an explanation of German unemployment over a time span of more than thirty years. This is a quite impressive attainment for such a simple model. If the story of this model is true, the simple reason for German unemployment is that average wages are too high, and this is due to the increase in wage taxes and social insurance contributions and the decrease of capital income taxation. The divergence between producer and consumer prices has worked in the opposite direction.

An important point to discuss is the significant influence of the capital income tax. As the results suggest the capital income tax has a significant influence on the employment rate which is in contrast to the prediction of the standard bargaining model with generalized Nash bargaining solution and capital income as firm utility. This is not a hard test, of course, since there are at least two caveats that can be made. First, the tax scheme for capital income taxation is not proportional in reality and changes in the average tax can be produced by nonproportional changes that may well have an influence on the solution in the Nash case. Second, one could think either of a more general functional form for firm utility that would allow for effects even of a proportional tax or simply of some other underlying concept than capital income. However, it was not the intention to discriminate between the two solutions empirically. As discussed in chapter 4 the Nash solution does not have empirically testable implications under general utility functions and a discrimination is therefore impossible. What is important here is that the model does not reject the proportional solution that does have testable implications.

What may be a bit surprising is that the elasticity of the capital income tax is much lower than the elasticity of the tax wedge, indicating that the capital income tax is only of minor importance in the firm utility. However, it might be that the real parameter of the capital income tax is higher, for two reasons:

1. There is the possibility of mismeasurement that could have biased the estimate downwards. As explained in the data section the variable chosen

is not exactly what one would have in mind from the theory. While the usual type of measurement error is not of importance asymptotically, because the consistency of the estimator is not affected, it might nonetheless have an effect in a small sample.

2. The assumptions on the functional forms of the utilities and/or the technology could be incorrect. If e.g. the technology is not Cobb-Douglas then the model is not loglinear any more, the parameter restrictions do not apply and the union or the firm utility could have a power different of one on wages or capital income. In this case the estimate would be a mixture of the real v and other parameters.

It should be noted here that a conspicuous argument that could be of importance is hard to justify in my opinion. It is the argument that high capital income taxes drive out capital, what leads to more unemployment because wages do not react enough. If this is true, then we would have two effects on employment of a higher taxation of capital. A positive one, because wages decrease according to the fairness considerations discussed above and a negative one, because labour productivity also decreases without an offsetting decrease in wages. If this argument is used to explain the trend in unemployment, then it violates the long-run neutrality of the capital stock towards employment. This is not a reasonable model of long-run employment determination. If the capital stock is really non-neutral towards employment and less capital means less employment, then from symmetry we should expect that more capital means more employment. But the capital stock clearly has a positive trend throughout the observation period and the result would be that this has tended to increase equilibrium employment in Germany. Then it would be even more difficult to explain why unemployment in Germany is so high. Maybe one could justify a negative impact of capital income taxation on employment by assuming that changes in the capital stock due to an increase in taxation have a different effect on wages than changes due to other factors. It is not clear why and how this should happen, however. Therefore, this only a weak argument for a lower positive effect of capital income taxation on employment.

The results of this chapter will be further discussed in the last chapter. An important point that is clarified in the next chapter is the question of whether the increase in the right hand side variables of the long-run model is caused by short-run deviations of the employment rate from its natural rate. If this is the case, then cyclical shocks play an important role in the explanation of the trend in German unemployment.

8. Hysteresis

Beginning with the paper of Blanchard and Summers (1986) the notion of hysteresis has gained prominence in the labour economics literature.[1] While it is generally sufficiently clear what is meant by hysteresis in a specific article, there are differences in the definition of the term between articles. In a loose fashion one could say that the term generally refers to a model where a shock can have a permanent effect.

The main reason for the popularity of this approach is the alleged failure of the variables in standard labour market models to account for the high levels of unemployment in Europe. As noted by Blanchard and Summers (1988): "We believe that understanding unemployment in Europe will require economists to dispense with the natural rate hypothesis that underlies much of both Keynesian and Classical macroeconomics. Theories of fragile equilibria are necessary to come to grip with events in Europe" (p.186). The econometric results in the last chapter show that this reasoning is not true for Germany. The estimated model is able to explain the rise in German unemployment in the last decades with variables from a simple bargaining model. Nonetheless, hysteresis might be of importance in Germany. How is this possible? To answer this question it is necessary to start with a closer examination of the concept of hysteresis and its implications for econometric modeling. This is done in the next section. In section 8.2 the relation between this discussion and earlier attempts to test for hysteresis in Germany is highlighted. Finally, section 8.3 evaluates the evidence for hysteresis in German unemployment with the derived framework.

8.1 Hysteresis Models

It is useful to discuss the different meanings of hysteresis as special properties of a prototypical model. A model generally describes a variable Y_t through a mathematical relation like

$$Y_t = f(\mathbf{x}_t) \tag{8.1}$$

[1] The idea as such can be found in a number of earlier contributions. See Røed (1997) for an overview.

where $\mathbf{x}_t \in \mathbf{X} \subset \mathbb{R}^N$ is a vector of N explanatory variables and $f(.)$ is a possibly multivalued function that associates each point in $\mathbf{X}$ with a set of points Y_t. Let's call $\mathbf{x}_t$ the structure and Y_t the equilibrium of the model at date t. If $f(.)$ is multivalued, this does not mean that the realization y_t of the endogenous variable itself is multivalued. The realization is assumed to be singlevalued, but it cannot be predicted by the structure of the model.

It is now possible to identify different frameworks for the mentioned path dependence effect. In the first one, discussed e.g. in Amable et al. (1993), $f(.)$ is multivalued. The model is derived from the origin of the term hysteresis in physics and the mathematical treatment in Krasnosel'skii and Pokrovskii (1989) and Mayergoyz (1991). Here, the realization at time t is determined by the history of the structure of the model. The concept distinguishes weak hysteresis that is observed on a micro level in so-called "elementary hysteretic operators", e.g. firms, and strong hysteresis that relates to the behaviour of aggregates of these micro units. The intuition behind weak hysteresis is the following. Assume that the structure is altered at time t such that the range of possible equilibria narrows to a single point $y_t = Y_t \in Y_{t-1}$ that is different from the realization in the period before y_{t-1}. This is called a "loading". In period $t+1$ the structure may revert to its former level in $t-1$, called "unloading", but there is no reason why the equilibrium should switch to its former level. In the examples given for this behaviour there is generally a kind of inertia involved that boils down to the assumption:

$$y_t \in Y_{t+1} \Rightarrow y_{t+1} = y_t \tag{8.2}$$

This behaviour of the microunits of the model leads to strong hysteresis of the aggregate. For an application of this model to trade see Baldwin and Krugman (1989). The model in this book is not of this type and therefore I want to concentrate on the other possible framework for hysteresis here.

Hysteresis is also an issue in linear models with unit roots (or zero roots in continuous time).[2] Consider the following univariate example

$$y_t = y_{t-1} + \boldsymbol{\beta}'\mathbf{x}_t + \epsilon_t \ , \tag{8.3}$$

where ϵ_t is a stationary stochastic process. In the deterministic model with $\epsilon_t = 0 \ \forall t$ the focus is on long-run equilibria of the type $\bar{Y} = f(\bar{\mathbf{x}})$, where $\bar{\mathbf{x}} = \lim_{t\to\infty} \mathbf{x}_t$ and $\bar{Y} = \lim_{t\to\infty} y_t$. Existence requires $\boldsymbol{\beta}'\bar{\mathbf{x}} = 0$. As Giavazzi and Wyplosz (1985) show for continuous time models, the steady state of y_t may be unique, but depends on the starting conditions and the parameters of the adjustment process. A brief discussion of the discrete case is given by Franz (1990). This behaviour is different from models with all roots inside the unit

[2] The difference to the mechanism described above is emphasized by Amable et al. (1993). They suggest that the use of the term hysteresis for the properties of linear models with unit roots is improper. I follow a large part of the literature here by using the term also for this class of models.

circle and the reason for the use of the term hysteresis model here. If y_t is not predetermined, i.e. if a starting value is not specified, the steady state is not unique. In the empirical hysteresis literature it is generally the stochastic model that is used, where y_t is a first order integrated process if $\boldsymbol{\beta}'\mathbf{x}_t$ is a stationary process. The difference is that even if the deterministic model has a steady state solution y_t has a stochastic trend in this model. This case is further discussed below.

The focus of this chapter is on the idea that this type of model is often the result of neglecting factors that are part of the "true" structure, but are not considered in the model, e.g. because they are unobservable. The hysteretic behaviour of the dependent variable could then be the result of permanent changes in these variables. If these changes are caused by past shocks to the dependent variable this is called "endogenous structural change" in the survey by Røed (1997). Røed emphasizes the importance of a discrimination between exogenous and endogenous structural changes in this respect. I want to show in the following that this idea is related to well established concepts in cointegration theory, that, to my knowledge, have not yet played a role in the literature on hysteresis.

Consider a model where $f(.)$ is a singlevalued function and y_t is predictable by $\mathbf{x}_t$ at every point in time. This is the sort of model that is generally in use in economics. Endogenous structural change is created by the fact that at least one of the $\mathbf{x}_t$ variables depends on past deviations from the equilibrium. In a linear model this can be written as

$$y_t = \boldsymbol{\beta}'\mathbf{x}_t + u_{1,t} \tag{8.4}$$

$$\boldsymbol{\Phi}(L)\mathbf{x}_t = \mathbf{v}_t \ , \tag{8.5}$$

where $\boldsymbol{\Phi}(L)$ is a matrix lag polynomial of unspecified order and $(u_{1,t}, \mathbf{v}_t')$ is a stationary vector stochastic process with

$$\mathrm{E}(\mathbf{v}_t | u_{1,t-1}, u_{1,t-2}, \dots) \neq \mathrm{E}(\mathbf{v}_t) \ . \tag{8.6}$$

Generally one would only speak of hysteresis if this change in the structure is permanent. If the change is not permanent, shocks eventually die out. One of the necessary conditions for this to hold is that the marginal process of the $\mathbf{x}_t$ variables is nonstationary, e.g. a first order integrated process. Under this assumption, and excluding the possibility of cointegration among these variables, the hysteresis model represents a cointegrated system with a single cointegration vector given by equation (8.4).

To illustrate the implications of hysteresis in a cointegration framework it is useful to go back to the triangular representation of a cointegrated system used in chapter 2:

$$y_t = \boldsymbol{\beta}'\mathbf{x}_t + u_{1,t} \tag{8.7}$$

$$\Delta\mathbf{x}_t = \mathbf{u}_{2,t} \ . \tag{8.8}$$

It is assumed that $\mathbf{u}_t' = (u_{1,t}, \mathbf{u}_{2,t}')$ follows a stationary linear process

$$\mathbf{B}(L)\mathbf{u}_t = \boldsymbol{\epsilon}_t \qquad \mathbf{B}(L) = \sum_{j=0}^{\infty} \mathbf{B}_j L^j, \quad \mathbf{B}_0 = \mathbf{I}_n , \tag{8.9}$$

where $\boldsymbol{\epsilon}_t$ is i.i.d. with mean zero and covariance matrix $\boldsymbol{\Sigma}$. The only difference here is that all the autocorrelation in the second equation is moved to the error term and only the unit root is left on the left hand side.

An important feature of this type of model is its observational equivalence with the other type of hysteresis model in equation (8.3) if one considers the reduced form of the model. As mentioned above, this might be necessary because the structural variables that are causing the dependence are unobservable. A reduced form would look like

$$\Delta y_t = \boldsymbol{\beta}' \mathbf{u}_{2,t} + \Delta u_{1,t} , \tag{8.10}$$

and therefore y_t contains a stochastic trend through $\mathbf{u}_{2,t}$. The analysis of reduced forms, without an effort to identify the important structural variables that produce the effect, is not a convincing procedure to test for hysteresis in this framework. Often the whole analysis boils down to a unit root test for y_t. However, such a test is not a sufficient indicator for the presence of hysteresis in this model, because shocks in equation (8.4) could have no permanent effect on the $\mathbf{x}_t$ variables and still the endogenous variable could have a unit root in its reduced form.

An important point to note is that the model does not necessarily imply hysteresis even if the right hand side variables depend on past equilibrium errors. To show this in more detail it is necessary to take a look on the structure of the error process. The following decomposition of a matrix lag polynomial will be useful

$$\begin{aligned} \mathbf{C}(L) &= \sum_{i=0}^{n} \mathbf{C}_i L^i \\ &= \sum_{i=0}^{n} \mathbf{C}_i L + (1-L)\mathbf{C}_0 + (1-L) \sum_{i=2}^{n} \left(\sum_{j=i}^{n} -\mathbf{C}_j \right) L^{i-1} , \end{aligned}$$

which can be written as

$$\mathbf{C}(L) = \mathbf{C}(1)L + (1-L)\mathbf{C}_0 + (1-L)\mathbf{C}^+(L) , \tag{8.11}$$

where $\mathbf{C}_i^+ = -\sum_{j=i+1}^{n} \mathbf{C}_j$ for $i = 1, \ldots, n-1$. This decomposition is now applied to the lag polynomial of the error process. First, rewrite (8.9) to

$$\mathbf{B}_1(L)u_{1,t} + \mathbf{B}_2(L)\mathbf{u}_{2,t} = \begin{pmatrix} \epsilon_{1,t} \\ \epsilon_{2,t} \end{pmatrix} , \tag{8.12}$$

where

$$\mathbf{B}_1(L) = \begin{pmatrix} b_{11}(L) \\ \mathbf{b}_{12}(L) \end{pmatrix} = \begin{pmatrix} 1 \\ \mathbf{0} \end{pmatrix} + \begin{pmatrix} b_{11,1} \\ \mathbf{b}_{12,1} \end{pmatrix} L + \ldots \tag{8.13}$$

$$\mathbf{B}_2(L) = \begin{pmatrix} \mathbf{b}_{21}(L) \\ \mathbf{B}_{22}(L) \end{pmatrix} = \begin{pmatrix} \mathbf{0}' \\ \mathbf{I} \end{pmatrix} + \begin{pmatrix} \mathbf{b}_{21,1} \\ \mathbf{B}_{22,1} \end{pmatrix} L + \ldots . \tag{8.14}$$

Using the introduced decomposition gives

$$\mathbf{B}_1(1)u_{1,t-1} + \begin{pmatrix} 1 \\ \mathbf{0} \end{pmatrix} \Delta u_{1,t} + \mathbf{B}_1^+(L)\Delta u_{1,t} + \mathbf{B}_2(L)\mathbf{u}_{2,t} = \begin{pmatrix} \epsilon_{1,t} \\ \boldsymbol{\epsilon}_{2,t} \end{pmatrix} . \tag{8.15}$$

Solving the last $n-1$ equations for $\mathbf{u}_{2,t}$ leads to

$$\Delta \mathbf{x}_t = -\mathbf{b}_{12}(1)u_{1,t-1} - \mathbf{b}_{12}^+(L)\Delta u_{1,t} - \mathbf{B}_{22}^*(L)\mathbf{u}_{2,t} + \boldsymbol{\epsilon}_{2,t} , \tag{8.16}$$

where $\mathbf{B}_{22}^*(L) = \mathbf{B}_{22}(L) - \mathbf{I}$. It is easily seen that a necessary and sufficient condition to have hysteresis in such a model is

$$-\mathbf{b}_{12}(1) \neq \mathbf{0} . \tag{8.17}$$

Only if this condition is satisfied, has a shock in the cointegration relation a long-run impact on the level of the right hand side variables. This condition is equivalent to weak exogeneity of the respective right hand side variables for the long-run parameters as can be shown in the following semi-structural form of the model:

$$\begin{aligned} \Delta y_t &= -b_{11}(1)(y_{t-1} - \boldsymbol{\beta}'\mathbf{x}_{t-1}) + \boldsymbol{\beta}'\Delta \mathbf{x}_t - b_{11}^+(L)\Delta y_t \\ &\quad + b_{11}^+(L)\boldsymbol{\beta}'\Delta \mathbf{x}_t - \mathbf{b}_{21}(L)\Delta \mathbf{x}_t + \epsilon_{1,t} \end{aligned} \tag{8.18}$$

$$\begin{aligned} \Delta \mathbf{x}_t &= -\mathbf{b}_{12}(1)(y_{t-1} - \boldsymbol{\beta}'\mathbf{x}_{t-1}) - \mathbf{b}_{12}^+(L)\Delta y_t \\ &\quad + \mathbf{b}_{12}^+(L)\boldsymbol{\beta}'\Delta \mathbf{x}_t - \mathbf{B}_{22}^*(L)\Delta \mathbf{x}_t + \boldsymbol{\epsilon}_{2,t} . \end{aligned} \tag{8.19}$$

As is well known (Boswijk, 1992; Urbain, 1993; Johansen, 1992), testing for weak exogeneity of a variable in this framework amounts to a test on the significance of the error correction term in the respective equation. For the $\mathbf{x}_t$ variables this is equivalent to the null hypothesis $-\mathbf{b}_{12}(1) = \mathbf{0}$. As a result, even if the endogenous variable has a unit root and there is feedback from the equilibrium error to the right hand side variables, this does not necessarily imply hysteresis. The key for getting stronger evidence on the presence of hysteresis is the error correction representation of the cointegration model.

Although the analysis so far concentrated on permanent effects of $u_{1,t}$, a definition of hysteresis based on permanent effects of $\epsilon_{1,t}$ would obviously lead to the same condition on the parameters. Since the model allows for contemporary correlation between $\epsilon_{1,t}$ and $\boldsymbol{\epsilon}_{2,t}$, the problem of identification of shocks that is pervasive in the literature on VAR models arises here as well. The stationary VAR that is of interest here is given by equation (8.9). One could argue that the partial impact of $\epsilon_{1,t}$ is not relevant, because the realization of $\epsilon_{1,t}$ contains information on the other error terms. However, I think that in the special framework discussed here it is adequate to define hysteresis with regard to the partial effect of $\epsilon_{1,t}$. If a structural shock were identified by an ordering of the variables, then it might be a reasonable assumption in many conceivable models of the natural rate that the variables determining the natural rate do only react with delay to disequilibrium errors, because these are generally variables that describe structural features of the economy. This would suggest the following structural form of the VAR

$$\boldsymbol{\Gamma}(L)\mathbf{u}_t = \tilde{\boldsymbol{\epsilon}}_t \qquad \boldsymbol{\Gamma}(L) = \sum_{j=0}^{\infty} \boldsymbol{\Gamma}_j L^j , \tag{8.20}$$

where the structural residuals $\tilde{\boldsymbol{\epsilon}}_t$ are i.i.d. with zero mean and diagonal covariance matrix $\tilde{\boldsymbol{\Sigma}}$ and

$$\boldsymbol{\Gamma}_0 = \begin{pmatrix} \gamma_{11} & \gamma_{21}' \\ \mathbf{0} & \boldsymbol{\Gamma}_{22} \end{pmatrix} . \tag{8.21}$$

If hysteresis were defined by the existence of a permanent impact of the structural residual $\tilde{\epsilon}_{1,t}$, again the same condition for hysteresis would result. Second, from the viewpoint of economic policy, the interesting question generally is whether a temporary change in the employment rate *without* changing the structural variables would induce a permanent reduction in the natural rate. Even if in the past the error terms were correlated, this does not preclude that economic policy can affect employment without changing the structure. And often it is argued that it is easier for policy to achieve employment effects through demand side policies than through structural reforms. Therefore, hysteresis as defined above seems to be the interesting case.

8.2 Relation to Previous Studies

In this section I want to compare the above framework with previous attempts to test for hysteresis. As should be clear from the discussion in the previous section, a unit root in the reduced form (un)employment relation is not necessarily an indication of hysteresis. It could be induced by exogenous variables containing a unit root in their marginal process. Therefore, tests that focus on the univariate properties of employment or unemployment like Wolters (1992) are not sufficiently informative for inference on hysteresis effects. This has been noticed by Jaeger and Parkinson (1994) who try to separate a cyclical component from the natural rate and test for repercussions of cyclical shocks to the natural rate. They find significant hysteresis effects for Germany in the sense that a one percent increase in the cyclical unemployment rate leads to a permanent increase of unemployment of 0.18 percent in Germany. Of course, their results rest upon the identification of the cyclical component through world demand movements. The model presented here can be seen as an alternative identification method using more economic theory.

A second line of research that should be mentioned here goes a step further and analyzes a specific source of hysteresis, namely wage setting by insiders, possibly represented by a trade union. This is the approach of Blanchard and Summers (1986), abbreviated by the symbol BS in the following discussion. They assume that the trade union sets wages as to reach a certain employment level that might depend on past employment, thereby introducing a persistence mechanism.[3] This leads to the following equilibrium relation for employment:

$$\mathrm{E}\, l_t = (1-a)l^* + a l_{t-1} \;, \tag{8.22}$$

where E is the expectations operator, l_t is the natural logarithm of employment in period t and l^* is a (constant) target level of employment. The parameter a is determining how much weight the union places on past employment, e.g. because of membership effects. It is this parameter that is estimated by BS to determine the degree of persistence in employment. Of course, testing for hysteresis, i.e. $a = 1$, using equation (8.22) would be a simple unit root test and subject to the criticism made above. However, in BS the parameter is not estimated from this equation, but from a modified wage equation. Labour demand in their model takes the form:

$$l_t = s * l_{t-1} - (1-s)b(w_t - p_t) + e_t \;, \tag{8.23}$$

where s characterizes partial adjustment, $w_t - p_t$ is the natural logarithm of the real wage, and e_t is an error term that follows a random walk: $e_t = e_{t-1} + \eta_t$. In this case wages will be set according to

$$w_t = \mathrm{E}\, p_t + \frac{(s-a)l_{t-1} - (1-a)l^* + \mathrm{E}\, e_t}{(1-s)b} \;. \tag{8.24}$$

Lagging equation (8.23) one period, solving for e_{t-1}, and substituting in this equation leads to the following equation that forms the basis of the estimates in BS and several other studies:

$$\Delta w_t = \mathrm{E}\, p_t - p_{t-1} + \frac{(1+s-a)l_{t-1} - s l_{t-2} - (1-a)l^*}{(1-s)b} \;. \tag{8.25}$$

The important implication of this equation is that in the case of $a = 1$ real wage growth depends on the change in past employment but not on the

[3] This model is a simple version of a richer class of so-called insider-outsider models. Important contributions to this theory have been made by Solow (1985) and Lindbeck and Snower (1986a,b, 1988).

level. In the opposite extreme of no persistence $a = 0$ the ratio of the absolute parameters on l_{t-1} and l_{t-2} cannot exceed 1/2. For Germany, the results in BS suggest that a is close to one, indicating hysteresis.

However, interpretation of the results is difficult. They depend heavily on the auxiliary assumptions of the model. As discussed in Lever (1995), the nature of the process for e_t is crucial for the relation between estimates and possible hysteresis effects. I come back to this point in the appendix. An even more problematic assumption concerns l^*. In the estimation, the assumption of a constant l^* is relaxed to a deterministic linear time trend[4] to proxy for changes in l^*. What they do not consider, however, is the possibility that l^* has a stochastic trend. The model presented in the previous chapters does not rely on insider effects. In the framework of BS it can be represented by an l^* that is determined by variables containing a stochastic trend and an a that is significantly below one. If a were close to one in Germany, as suggested by the estimation in BS, the model would take the form in (8.3) and it would have been impossible to find a cointegration relation in this model. Therefore, the BS model cannot explain the existence of this long-run relation. The important question is whether the model of this book is able to explain the BS results. This would support this model because it encompasses the BS model in the sense of Mizon and Richard (1986).

Assume that $l^* = x_t$ and, for simplicity, $x_t = x_{t-1} + v_t$, where v_t is a stationary stochastic process. To interpret the BS results it is important to determine the effect of neglecting x_t in the estimated equation. From equations (8.23) and (8.24) it follows that:

$$\begin{aligned} l_t &= (1-a)x_t + al_{t-1} + e_t - \mathrm{E}\, e_t - (1-s)b(\mathrm{E}\, p_t - p_t) \Leftrightarrow \\ x_t &= \frac{1}{1-a}(l_t - \eta_t - al_{t-1} + (1-s)b(\mathrm{E}\, p_t - p_t)) \\ &= \frac{1}{1-a}(l_{t-1} - \eta_{t-1} - al_{t-2} + (1-s)b(\mathrm{E}\, p_{t-1} - p_{t-1})) + v_t \,. \end{aligned} \tag{8.26}$$

This can now be substituted in equation (8.25) leading to

$$\Delta w_t = \mathrm{E}\, p_t - \mathrm{E}\, p_{t-1} + \frac{(s-a)l_{t-1} - (s-a)l_{t-2} - (1-a)v_t + \eta_{t-1}}{(1-s)b} \,. \tag{8.27}$$

As can easily be seen, the ratio of the parameters before l_{t-1} and l_{t-2} is now equal to one in absolute terms irrespective of the true value of a. The parameters are not estimated consistently, because the error term is correlated with one of the regressors. Nonetheless, this strongly indicates that the interpretation of the results in BS is not robust to assumptions about the process generating l^*.

[4] This is extended to a deterministic quadratic time trend in Alogoskoufis and Manning (1988).

8.3 Hysteresis in German Unemployment

The model that was estimated in section 7.3 can be seen as a model of the natural rate of employment. Hysteresis could play a role in this model only if one of the right hand side variables depends on past equilibrium errors in the way described above. If there were hysteresis because of some other unobserved variable this would imply the absence of cointegration between the variables in the model. Because this is not the case, the results reduce the number of possible variables that produce a hysteresis effect sharply.

Only the observed variables are candidates in this case. The usual factors that are mentioned in the literature (see e.g. Hargreaves, 1980; Carlin and Soskice, 1990) like union membership, capital scrapping by firms or skill losses of the unemployed do not play a role here. The variable that is included in the model and is most likely to depend on past unemployment is the tax wedge that includes the social insurance contributions. The story behind this effect is quite simple: if a shock leads to a negative deviation of the employment rate from the natural rate, this could lead to an increase of contribution rates, especially for unemployment insurance, of the workers still employed and this will be of importance in the wage negotiations, where the union will manage to push wages up, which stabilizes the lower employment rate.

To explore this possibility further the natural starting point is again a seasonal ECM for the series, as in chapter 5 that can be seen as a reduced form of the model in equations (8.18) and (8.19):

$$\begin{aligned}\Delta_4 \mathbf{z}_t = \boldsymbol{\Pi}_1 \mathbf{w}_{1,t-1} + \boldsymbol{\Pi}_2 \mathbf{w}_{2,t-1} + \boldsymbol{\Pi}_3 \mathbf{w}_{3,t-1} + \boldsymbol{\Pi}_4 \mathbf{w}_{3,t} \\ + \mathbf{A}_1 \Delta_4 \mathbf{z}_{t-1} + \cdots + \mathbf{A}_p \Delta_4 \mathbf{z}_{t-p} + \bar{\boldsymbol{\epsilon}}_t \,, \end{aligned} \tag{8.28}$$

where

$$\mathbf{w}_{1,t} = (1 + L + L^2 + L^3)\mathbf{z}_t \tag{8.29}$$
$$\mathbf{w}_{2,t} = (1 - L + L^2 - L^3)\mathbf{z}_t \tag{8.30}$$
$$\mathbf{w}_{3,t} = (L - L^3)\mathbf{z}_t \tag{8.31}$$

and the $\bar{\boldsymbol{\epsilon}}_t$ are n.i.i.d. with mean zero and covariance matrix $\bar{\boldsymbol{\Sigma}}$. The vector $\mathbf{z}_t$ is given by

$$\mathbf{z}_t = (\ln e_t, \ln pw_t, \ln tw_t, \ln(1 - t_{pt}))' \,. \tag{8.32}$$

In light of the different behaviour of the series in the univariate seasonal integration tests, one cannot assume that all seasonal unit roots are present in the series. I therefore collected the variables that have a seasonal unit root at a certain frequency in a separate model and conducted trace tests for seasonal cointegration according to Lee (1992). The results are given in table 8.1. The estimations included a constant and seasonal dummies. At frequency $\omega = \pi/2$ the analysis is restricted to the case of contemporaneous cointegration. The critical values for the case $r = 0$ have been simulated using the random number generator of GAUSS with 30000 replications of the process $\Delta_4 \mathbf{x}_t = \epsilon_t$ with ϵ_t i.i.d. $N(\mathbf{0}, \mathbf{I})$ and 130 observations. For the case $r = 1$ the critical values are taken from Lee and Siklos (1995).

Table 8.1. Trace tests

H_0	Π_2	Π_3
$(\ln e_t, \ln pw_t, \ln tw_t)$		
r=0	25.71	46.60**
r=1	10.10	17.87
$(\ln pw_t, \ln tw_t, \ln(1 - t_{pt}))$		
r=0	19.93	57.41**
r=1	9.76	27.00**

* 10% sig., ** 5% sig.

The tests for cointegration at the seasonal frequencies led to results that were not always in line with the results of the univariate tests in chapter 7. For the first vector considered $(\ln e_t, \ln pw_t, \ln tw_t)'$ the null hypothesis of no seasonal cointegration was only rejected for the frequency $\omega = \pi/2$, which is easily explained by the fact that $\ln e_t$ does not have a unit root at this frequency according to the univariate tests. In the ECM I therefore included $(1 - L^2) \ln e_{t-1}$ and $(1 - L^2) \ln e_{t-2}$ as regressors. Further, the tests indicate the existence of two cointegration vectors for $(\ln pw_t, \ln tw_t, \ln(1 - t_{pt}))$ at the frequency $\omega = \pi/2$. However, despite the fact that $\ln(1 - t_{pt})$ does not have a unit root at this frequency in the univariate test, the tests did not reject the null hypothesis at the frequency $\omega = \pi$. I decided to follow the univariate results and included $(1 - L)(1 + L^2) \ln(1 - t_{pt-1})$ in the model. Regarding the conflicting results for $\ln pw_t$ in the univariate tests, the existence of seasonal cointegration could partially be due to the fact that $\ln pw_t$ has nearly a unit root. This is also reflected by an estimate of $(126.41, 10.07, 7.98)$ for the first cointegration vector. Therefore, I simply put $(1 - L^2) \ln pw_{t-1}$ and $(1 - L^2) \ln pw_{t-2}$ in the regression. This restriction of the cointegration space was confirmed by a separate trace test for the last two variables which have the cointegration vector $\gamma_1 = (-71.01, 15.76)'$ leading to the inclusion of $\gamma_1'(1 - L^2)\mathbf{z}_{1t-2} = \gamma_1'(1 - L^2)(\ln tw_{t-2}, \ln(1 - t_{pt-2}))'$. All the series were adjusted for remaining deterministic seasonality. It must be emphasized that the results presented below are not very sensitive to the exclusion of one or several of these terms and the main conclusions are very robust.

The cointegration vector at the zero frequency is estimated by maximum likelihood, and the ECM is estimated by OLS. Both estimations included an intercept that is not reported. Considering a maximum length of eight, the SIC criterion suggests the use of one lag in the estimation. Lag lengths of two and three have the second and third best values respectively. The estimated cointegration vectors are given in table 8.2. It is interesting that the results are quite close to the results using the fully modified procedure. The results for the ECM using one lag are given in table 8.3, the results with two and three lags in table 8.4. As can be seen, except for the price wedge in the model with two and three lags, all right hand side variables are weakly exogenous. The result concerning the price wedge is not robust. With more than three lags the result vanishes again. Taken together, I conclude from the results that the null hypothesis of no hysteresis is not rejected by this model for the tax wedge and the capital income tax. The evidence for hysteresis effects through the price wedge is only weak. This indicates that feedback effects of deviations from the natural rate to the natural rate itself through contribution rates for unemployment insurance do not exist.

Table 8.2. Cointegration vectors

	$\Delta_4 \ln e_t$	$\Delta_4 \ln pw_t$	$\Delta_4 \ln tw_t$	$\Delta_4 \ln(1-t_{pt})$
1 lag	1.000	−0.525**	0.443**	0.132**
2 lags	1.000	−0.551**	0.456**	0.115**
3 lags	1.000	−0.544**	0.437**	0.158**

* 10% sig., ** 5% sig.

Table 8.3. ECM with one lag

	Dependent variable			
	$\Delta_4 \ln e_t$	$\Delta_4 \ln pw_t$	$\Delta_4 \ln tw_t$	$\Delta_4 \ln(1-t_{pt})$
$\gamma' \mathbf{z}_{t-1}$	−0.051**	0.042	−0.018	−0.006
$\Delta_4 \ln e_{t-1}$	0.657**	0.051	−0.080	−1.18**
$\Delta_4 \ln pw_{t-1}$	−0.029	0.474**	−0.080	0.299
$\Delta_4 \ln tw_{t-1}$	0.017	0.016	0.587**	−0.250*
$\Delta_4 \ln(1-t_{pt-1})$	0.000	−0.029	0.134**	0.255**
$(1-L^2)\ln e_{t-1}$	0.217**	0.316**	0.124	0.279
$(1-L^2)\ln e_{t-2}$	0.073	−0.243*	0.030	0.337
$\Delta(1+L^2)\ln(1-t_{pt-1})$	0.003	0.007	−0.018	0.100**
$(1-L^2)\ln pw_{t-1}$	−0.017	0.089*	−0.162**	0.121
$(1-L^2)\ln pw_{t-2}$	0.030**	0.250**	−0.015	0.023
$\gamma_1'(1-L^2)\mathbf{z}_{1t-2}$	0.000	0.000	−0.003**	0.003**

* 10% sig., ** 5% sig.

A possible explanation lies in the nature of adjustments to this variable. The contribution rates for unemployment insurance are not changed immediately if the employment rate deviates from the long-run level. Cyclical swings

Table 8.4. ECM with 2 and 3 lags

	Dependent variable				Dependent variable			
	$\Delta_4 \ln e_t$	$\Delta_4 \ln pw_t$	$\Delta_4 \ln tw_t$	$\Delta_4 \ln(1-t_{pt})$	$\Delta_4 \ln e_t$	$\Delta_4 \ln pw_t$	$\Delta_4 \ln tw_t$	$\Delta_4 \ln(1-t_{pt})$
$\gamma' \mathbf{z}_{t-1}$	−0.039**	0.049*	0.020	0.022	−0.044**	0.064**	0.072	0.004
$\Delta_4 \ln e_{t-1}$	0.898**	0.317	0.455	−0.666	0.945**	0.232	0.520	−0.801
$\Delta_4 \ln pw_{t-1}$	0.008	0.471**	0.235	0.412	0.006	0.462**	0.140	0.419
$\Delta_4 \ln tw_{t-1}$	0.014	−0.014	0.613**	−0.379**	0.025	−0.024	0.582**	−0.363**
$\Delta_4 \ln(1-t_{pt-1})$	−0.001	−0.004	0.049	0.244**	0.005	−0.010	0.041	0.248**
$\Delta_4 \ln e_{t-2}$	−0.265**	−0.294	−0.498	−0.545	−0.492**	−0.077	0.041	−0.562
$\Delta_4 \ln pw_{t-2}$	−0.024	0.002	−0.068	−0.171	−0.038	−0.042	−0.135	−0.246
$\Delta_4 \ln tw_{t-2}$	−0.017	0.085	−0.219**	0.220	−0.010	0.186**	−0.210*	0.398*
$\Delta_4 \ln(1-t_{pt-2})$	−0.015	−0.039	0.081*	0.024	−0.016	−0.044	0.047	0.007
$\Delta_4 \ln e_{t-3}$					0.180*	−0.151	−0.547	0.154
$\Delta_4 \ln pw_{t-3}$					0.000	0.089	0.180	0.066
$\Delta_4 \ln tw_{t-3}$					0.000	−0.172**	−0.050	−0.266
$\Delta_4 \ln(1-t_{pt-3})$					0.011	−0.031	0.018	−0.020
$(1-L^2) \ln e_{t-1}$	0.183**	0.308**	−0.057	0.257	0.200**	0.306**	−0.088	0.277
$(1-L^2) \ln e_{t-2}$	0.097**	−0.211	0.070	0.376	0.112**	−0.274*	−0.090	0.320
$\Delta(1+L^2) \ln(1-t_{pt-1})$	0.002	0.002	−0.010	0.098**	0.002	0.000	−0.013	0.095**
$(1-L^2) \ln pw_{t-1}$	−0.020	0.095*	−0.185**	0.138	−0.019	0.122*	−0.118	0.168
$(1-L^2) \ln pw_{t-2}$	0.032**	0.248**	−0.024	−0.009	0.037**	0.246	−0.008	−0.005
$\gamma_1'(1-L^2)\mathbf{z}_{1t-2}$	0.000	0.000	−0.003**	0.004**	0.000	0.000	−0.003**	0.004**

* 10% sig., ** 5% sig.

in the amount of paid unemployment benefits can be accommodated by the Federal Labour Office by financial support from the government. The federal government in Germany is obliged by law (Art.120 GG) to defray any deficits in the budget of the Federal Labour Office. These contributions of the government have a strong cyclical component and made up a large part of the increase in spending on unemployment insurance after the two oil price shocks (Dornbusch, 1991). It should not be concluded, however, that contribution rates are independent of the employment rate. After all, contribution rates for unemployment insurance have increased from 2% in 1960 to 6.5% in 1993 in Germany and this is clearly related to the trend in the unemployment rate. This suggests that the contribution rate is only increased if there are signs of a permanent change in the employment rate which necessitates an increase in average contributions. Although this seems to be an intuitive argument, there are other possible interpretations of the results.

On the one hand, it should be noted that contributions to unemployment insurance play only a minor role in the overall tax wedge. Between 1960 and 1993 the contribution rates for health insurance increased from 8.4% to 13.4%, the contribution rate for the state pension system from 14% to 17.5% and, most important, the average wage tax increased from 5% to 20%.[5] The contributions of the unemployed for health care and, since 1978, for the pension system are paid by the Federal Labour Office from the contributions to unemployment insurance. Increases in these contribution rates to social insurance are therefore possibly due to other factors than unemployment. As a result, the feedback effects through the tax wedge caused by deviations from the natural rate are perhaps too small to be significant.

On the other hand, one could argue that the ECM framework is not appropriate for describing adjustments to contribution rates. For example the assumption, implicit in the dynamic model, that contribution rates are adjusted frequently is perhaps unrealistic. In contrast to the explanation given above, this could invalidate the results. To shed light on this argument it is useful to take a more direct route of detecting a causality between the employment rate and contribution rates. A natural framework for this question is a VAR for the yearly growth rate of average contribution rates to social insurance $\Delta_4 \ln ss_t$ and the yearly growth rate of the employment rate $\Delta_4 \ln e_t$. In figure 8.1 the p-values for recursive Granger causality tests are plotted. The null hypothesis is that the parameters of all lags of $\Delta_4 \ln e_t$ are zero in the equation for $\Delta_4 \ln ss_t$. All samples start in 1961:1 and end in the quarter indicated on the horizontal axis. The VAR included a constant and three lags. The results for two and four lags are quite similar, however. The results show highly significant p-values for all samples that comprise more than fourteen years of data. Therefore, the employment rate Granger causes

[5] The average wage tax rates are from the national accounts of the DIW. The social insurance contribution rates are taken from: Institut der deutschen Wirtschaft Köln (1996).

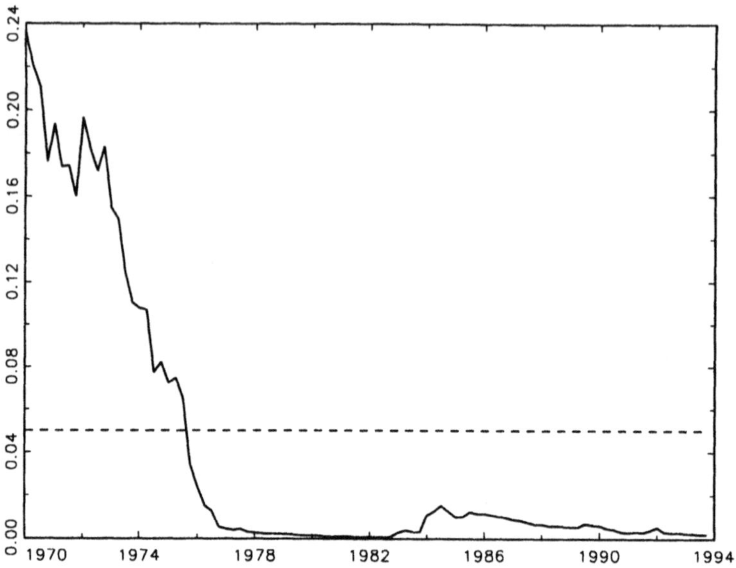

Fig. 8.1. P-values for recursive Granger causality tests

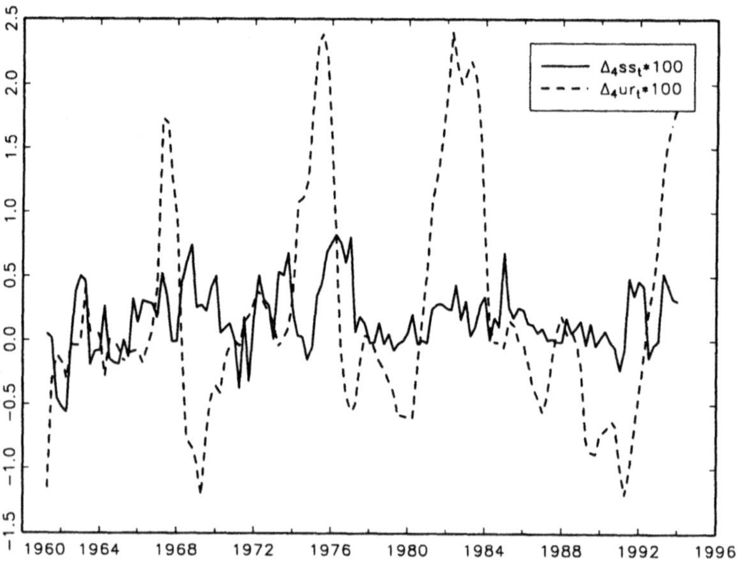

Fig. 8.2. Contribution rates and unemployment rate

social insurance contributions even with quite short samples. This suggests two things. First, the chosen dynamic statistical representation captures this dependence quite well, and the exogeneity result in the ECM is therefore unlikely to be an artifact of an inappropriate econometric procedure. Second, the high significance is an indication that at least social insurance contributions are quite sensitive to the employment rate. This is also suggested by the plot of the changes in the unemployment rate $\Delta_4 ur_t$ and the changes in average contribution rates $\Delta_4 ss_t$ in figure 8.2. As can be seen, there is an above average increase in contribution rates after the first two recessions and a less pronounced one after the second oil price shock. This is in line with the argument made above that changes in the long-run level of the employment rate do affect contribution rates. Changes in the employment rate are at least a noisy signal of changes in the long-run level of the employment rate and therefore the VAR model produces significant results.

In sum, the results of the estimations suggest that deviations from the natural rate do not induce significant shifts in the right hand side variables. Only if there are increases in the natural rate, might this have repercussions on other variables on the right hand side that reinforce this trend. The next and last chapter summarizes and evaluates these findings from a policy perspective.

9. Conclusions

What are the conclusions from the analysis in this book? The answer to this question clearly depends on the confidence one has in the empirical results presented. Everyone doing empirical research in economics knows that what seemed to be a perfectly convincing result at a certain point of time is often seen as an unsatisfactory description of the world only a few important articles later. The most prominent example is perhaps the Phillips curve (Phillips, 1958). This does not mean that empirical research is worthless, of course. Empirical evidence is a major driving force behind scientific progress in economics. It is the interplay between empirical results and theoretical explanations that often leads to the most interesting and stimulating discussions within the profession. An important example of this process is again the Phillips curve. And in this respect the results of this book should be seen as a contribution to the discussion surrounding the German and even the European unemployment problem. The model presented in this book is not the first explanation of German unemployment that has been suggested, and it will certainly not be the last. It is important because it emphasizes an aspect of the problem that has not been given enough attention in the past. And the empirical evidence in favor of this explanation is strong enough to take the issue seriously. As in every study that puts the focus on a special feature of the economy, several other aspects are neglected. Because it is an aggregate model, any effects of wage dispersion are assumed away.[1] Further, as discussed at several places, any influence of technological progress on equilibrium unemployment is ruled out. This contrasts with a strand of the literature where skill-biased technological change serves as an explanation for the high unemployment rates among unskilled workers.[2] These are only two examples of a long list of arguments that have been put forward in the literature (see Nickell, 1990, for a survey). However, it is generally not possible to consider all possible explanations in a unified model and one has to concentrate on only some aspects of a problem, like in this book.

[1] For an overview of the discussion, see the papers collected in Freeman and Katz (1995).

[2] For international evidence on skill-biased technological change, see Berman et al. (1998) and Machin and Van Reenen (1998).

Nonetheless, this chapter presents recommendations for economic policy using the simple framework developed in this book. This would at least ensure that economic policy is carried out according to a consistent empirically tested model, which should be a reasonable requirement, but seems to be a rare case in reality. The policy implications derived here are not based on a comprehensive welfare analysis, of course. It is assumed that the goal is a reduction in the unemployment rate. A decision of which of the possible measures to achieve this is preferable from the viewpoint of overall welfare is not possible with the model of this book. Since this book is only concerned with unemployment in Germany, the policy implications are also tailored to the German situation. The German government changed in 1998. The new government has already launched a tax reform aimed at reducing the number of unemployed in Germany. What are the implications of the econometric results derived here for the likely impact of this reform and other proposed policy measures on the unemployment rate?

The results of this book indicate that the increase in unemployment is caused mainly by exogenous policy variables like taxes and social insurance contributions. An important factor is the tax wedge between labour costs and net wages. This wedge has increased dramatically over the last decades in West Germany, and it is one of the conspicuous reasons for the very high labour costs in West Germany compared to other European countries. As a consequence, various measures that would lower the wedge have been suggested by politicians and also by the new government. A first step in this direction is the reduction of contribution rates for the pension system. This measure is part of the ecological tax reform that in turn increases energy taxes to finance these reductions. An important question for the evaluation of this reform is whether the increase in energy taxes will lead to negative employment effects that would make the overall impact on unemployment ambiguous. One effect of an energy tax on the part of the firms should be an increase in the after tax price of this input. The aggregate model of this book would predict that energy taxes do not change the equilibrium employment rate through this channel, because wages adapt to changes in factor prices, offsetting any effect on employment. With the Cobb-Douglas technology used in the model, all factor inputs are price substitutes. Nonetheless, if output is not fixed, an increase in a factor price leads to a decrease in output and a decrease in all factor inputs. As a result, wages would decrease in this model, leaving equilibrium employment unchanged. On the other hand, the energy tax could also have an effect on the price wedge, because it is likely to affect producer as well as consumer prices. The direction of this effect, however, is difficult to evaluate and even a tentative conclusion is beyond the scope of the informal discussion here.

Another important tax variable is capital income taxation. From the logic of the model it would be a good idea to increase taxes on capital income to finance the reductions in the tax wedge. The same recommendation is derived by Koskela and Schöb (1998) in a different model, where the wage is either assumed fix or is determined by a union-firm bargain using the Nash solution. However, in their model, in the Cobb-Douglas case, only a tax reform that does both, increase the tax on capital income and reduce the tax on wages will lead to more employment. The result of this book is different because even a higher taxation of capital alone would induce positive employment effects. This increase in capital income taxation could be achieved for example by abolishing the discrimination of investment in financial capital in Germany, caused by different forms of accelerated depreciation and investment tax credits that are granted for investment in physical capital as discussed by Sinn (1997).

A further result that is of great importance for the policy discussion is the insignificance of the labour supply variable. This variable is clearly to some extent a policy variable, because the timing of retirement, the time spent in education, immigration and other important factors are heavily dependent on government policy. If the unemployment rate is reduced by such a policy the fact that the wage might react to this must be taken into account. For instance, if the age for retirement is reduced, as is regularly suggested by German politicians, this will lead to the replacement of old workers with younger ones thereby reducing the unemployment rate for a given employment level. However, according to my estimates, this will not lower the long-run level of the unemployment rate, because wages will increase and exactly offset any effect on the unemployment rate by reducing labour demand. This result adds another argument against such policies. It is well known that Germany, like many other industrialized countries, has a demographic problem caused by decreasing birth rates that will lead to an increase in future contribution rates to the pay-as-you-go state pension system.[3] The reduction in labour supply through early retirement leads to a decrease in employment and an increase in the number of pensioners. It therefore decreases the number of employed that have to pay for one pensioner and exacerbates the already precarious situation in the pension system. The estimated model predicts even more wage pressure and unemployment in such a scenario because rising contribution rates increase the tax wedge. The recommendation for policy is therefore that the retirement age should be increased, not the reverse.

The important message from chapter 8 is that any measures that have only temporary effects on economic activity, for example because of nominal rigidities, do not lead to a permanent reduction in unemployment through structural changes shifting the natural rate. This contrasts with the predictions of standard hysteresis models. Therefore, shocks from monetary policy do not change the natural rate, and we cannot hope that lower interest rates by the ECB are useful for curing the structural unemployment problems in

[3] For projections of the contribution rates to the German pension system in different scenarios see Wissenschaftlicher Beirat beim Bundesministerium für Wirtschaft (1998) and Schnabel (1998).

Germany. Of course this does not mean that there are no cyclical effects on employment of lower interest rates. From a long-run perspective, however, this is not helpful and may even be counterproductive if as a consequence of a temporary reduction in unemployment necessary and possibly painful reforms are not undertaken.

Finally, the question arises as to whether the euro is going to solve the problem. The fiscal and monetary prudence in all European countries after the Maastricht treaty caused a marked decrease in nominal and real interest rates in Europe, to some extent even in Germany. According to the efficiency wage models in Phelps (1994), permanently lower real interest rates should reduce the equilibrium unemployment rate. The result in chapter 5, however, indicates that Germany is not in an efficiency wage regime and that we should analyze the possible impact of this development in a union bargaining framework. In the model of this book the interest rate does not play a role for unemployment determination. Its influence on the user costs of capital may lead to a change in the capital stock, but this does not affect unemployment because of the assumption of long-run neutrality. As long as the interest rate does not significantly influence any of the price or tax variables entering the equation for the employment rate, which is uncertain, it will not contribute to a reduction in unemployment. The conclusion from this study is therefore that the German government cannot hope to avoid painful reforms because the euro will solve the problem anyway. Without fast and radical treatment it is likely that the current trend in the variables determining the natural rate continues at least in the near future and unemployment in Germany will rise from one business cycle to the next just as it did in the last thirty years.

Often in economics it takes years until new insights make their way into the minds of politicians and actually influence economic policy. Regarding the main conclusions drawn from the analysis in this book, however, this might be one of the rare examples where it is not necessary to be that patient. I end this book with a few sentences of the German minister of economics Werner Müller from an interview with the German weekly DIE ZEIT, no.8, January 18th 1999, p.21, with the title: "We need more justice". He said: "Further, I see a major gap in justice [...] The state is getting ever more expensive. This is financed predominantly by the factor labour. This has contributed to the increase in unemployment. We have to stop this unfortunate spiral" (translation by the author).

Author Index

Subject Index

Bibliography

Abeysinghe, T. (1994). Deterministic seasonal models and spurious regressions. *Journal of Econometrics 61*, 259–272.

Akerlof, G. A. (1982). Labor contracts as partial gift exchange. *Quarterly Journal of Economics 97*, 543–569.

Alexander, C. O. (1992). The Kalai-Smorodinsky bargaining solution in wage negotiations. *Journal of the Operational Research Society 43*, 779–786.

Alexander, C. O. and W. Ledermann (1994). The constrained Nash bargaining solution. *Journal of the Operational Research Society 45*, 954–958.

Alexander, C. O. and W. Ledermann (1996). Are Nash bargaining wage agreements unique? An investigation into bargaining sets for firm-union negotiations. *Oxford Economic Papers 48*, 242–253.

Alogoskoufis, G. and A. Manning (1988). Wage setting and unemployment persistence in Europe, Japan and the USA. *European Economic Review 32*, 698–706.

Alogoskoufis, G. and A. Manning (1991). Tests of alternative wage employment bargaining models with an application to the UK aggregate labour market. *European Economic Review 35*, 23–37.

Amable, B., J. Henry, F. Lordon, and R. Topol (1993). Unit-root in the wage-price spiral is not hysteresis in unemployment. *Journal of Economic Studies 20*, 123–135.

Andrews, D. (1991). Heteroscedasticity and autocorrelation consistent covariance estimation. *Econometrica 59*, 817–858.

Baldwin, R. and P. Krugman (1989). Persistent trade effects of large exchange rate shocks. *Quarterly Journal of Economics 104*, 636–654.

Banerjee, A., J. J. Dolado, D. F. Hendry, and G. W. Smith (1986). Exploring equilibrium relationships in econometrics through static models: Some monte carlo evidence. *Oxford Bulletin of Economics and Statistics 48*, 253–277.

Berman, E., J. Bound, and S. Machin (1998). Implications of skill-biased technological change: International evidence. *Quarterly Journal of Economics 113*, 1245–1279.

Bils, M. J. (1985). Real wages over the business cycle: Evidence from panel data. *Journal of Political Economy 93*, 666–689.

Binmore, K., A. Rubinstein, and A. Wolinsky (1986). The Nash bargaining solution in economic modelling. *RAND Journal of Economics 17(2)*, 176–188.

Blanchard, O. J. and S. Fischer (1989). *Lectures on Macroeconomics.* Cambridge, Mass. and London: MIT Press.

Blanchard, O. J. and L. H. Summers (1986). Hysteresis and the European unemployment problem. In S. Fischer (Ed.), *NBER Macroeconomics Annual 1986*, Cambridge, Mass. and London, pp. 15–89. MIT Press.

Blanchard, O. J. and L. H. Summers (1988). Beyond the natural rate hypothesis. *American Economic Review 78*, 182–187.

Booth, A. L. (1995). *The Economics of the Trade Union.* Cambridge: Cambridge University Press.

Boswijk, P. H. (1992). *Cointegration, Identification and Exogeneity: Inference in Structural Error Correction Models.* Amsterdam: Thesis Publishers.

Bowles, S. (1985). The production process in a competitive economy: Walrasian, neo-Hobbesian, and Marxian models. *American Economic Review 75*, 16–36.

Brown, R., J. Durbin, and J. Evans (1975). Techniques for testing the constancy of regression relationships over time. *Journal of the Royal Statistical Society 37*, 149–172.

Bulkley, G. and G. D. Myles (1996). Trade unions, efficiency wages, and shirking. *Oxford Economic Papers 48*, 75–88.

Calvo, G. (1979). Quasi-walrasian theories of unemployment. *American Economic Review 69*, 102–107.

Canova, F. and B. E. Hansen (1995). Are seasonal patterns constant over time? A test for seasonal stability. *Journal of Business & Economic Statistics 13(3)*, 237–252.

Carlin, W. and D. Soskice (1990). *Macroeconomics and the Wage Bargain: A Modern Approach to Employment, Inflation, and the Exchange Rate.* Oxford: Oxford University Press.

Carruth, A. and C. Schnabel (1993). The determination of contract wages in West Germany. *Scandinavian Journal of Economics 95(3)*, 297–310.

Cartter, A. M. (1959). *Theory of Wages and Employment.* Homewood: Irwin.

Conley, J. P. and S. Wilkie (1996). An extension of the Nash bargaining solution to nonconvex problems. *Games and Economic Behaviour 13*, 26–38.

Darby, J. and S. Wren-Lewis (1993). Is there a cointegrating vector for UK wages? *Journal of Economic Studies 20,1/2*, 87–115.

de Menil, G. (1971). *Bargaining: Monopoly Power versus Union Power.* Cambridge, Mass.: MIT Press.

Dickey, D. A. and W. A. Fuller (1979). Distribution of the estimators for autoregressive time series with a unit root. *Journal of the American Statistical Association 74*, 427–431.

Dornbusch, H.-L. (1991). *Finanzprobleme der Arbeitslosenversicherung.* Bonn: Institut "Finanzen und Steuern".

Dunlop, J. T. (1938). The movement of real and money wage rates. *Economic Journal 48*, 413–434.

Dunlop, J. T. (1950). *Wage Determination Under Trade Unions.* New York: Kelley.

Durbin, J. (1970). Testing for serial correlation in least-squares regression when some of the regressors are lagged dependent variables. *Econometrica 38*, 410–421.

Engle, R. F. and C. W. J. Granger (1987). Co-integration and error correction: Representation, estimation and testing. *Econometrica 55*, 251–276.

Engle, R. F., C. W. J. Granger, and J. J. Hallman (1989). Merging short- and long-run forecasts: An application of seasonal cointegration to monthly electricity sales forecasting. *Journal of Econometrics 40*, 45–62.

Engle, R. F., C. W. J. Granger, S. Hylleberg, and H. S. Lee (1993). Seasonal cointegration: The Japanese consumption function. *Journal of Econometrics 55*, 275–298.

Fedeli, S. (1994). Testing a model of trade union behaviour: An application of a multivariate cointegration analysis to UK aggregate wage data. *Labour 8(1)*, 99–142.

Fellner, W. (1947). Prices and wages under bilateral monopoly. *Quarterly Journal of Economics 61*, 503–532.

Flaig, G. and V. Steiner (1993). Searching for the "productivity slowdown": Some surprising findings from West German manufacturing. *Review of Economics and Statistics 75*, 57–65.

Franses, P. H. (1996). *Periodicity and Stochastic Trends in Economic Time Series.* Oxford: Oxford University Press.

Franz, W. (1990). Hysteresis in economic relationships: An overview. In W. Franz (Ed.), *Hysteresis Effects in Economic Models*, pp. 1–17. Heidelberg: Physica.

Freeman, R. B. and L. F. Katz (Eds.) (1995). *Differences and Changes in Wage Structures*, Chicago and London. University of Chicago Press.

Friedman, M. (1968). The role of monetary policy. *American Economic Review 58*, 1–17.

Garman, D. M. and D. J. Richards (1992). Wage-price flexibility, market power, and the cyclical behaviour of real wages, 1959-1980. *The Quarterly Journal of Economics 107*, 1437–1449.

Geary, P. T. and J. Kennan (1982). The employment-real wage relationship: An international study. *Journal of Political Economy 90*, 854–871.

Ghysels, E., H. S. Lee, and P. L. Siklos (1993). On the (mis)specification of seasonality and its consequences: An empirical investigation with US data. *Empirical Economics 18*, 747–760.

Ghysels, E. and P. Perron (1993). The effect of seasonal adjustment filters on tests for a unit root. *Journal of Econometrics 55*, 57–98.

Giavazzi, F. and C. Wyplosz (1985). The zero root problem: A note on the dynamics of the stationary equilibrium in linear models. *Review of Economic Studies 52*, 353–357.

Giersch, H., K.-H. Paqué, and H. Schmieding (1992). *The fading miracle: Four decades of market economy in Germany*. Cambridge: Cambridge University Press.

Granger, C. W. J. and P. Newbold (1974). Spurious regressions in econometrics. *Journal of Econometrics 2*, 111–120.

Grout, P. A. (1984). Investment and wages in the absence of binding contracts: A Nash bargainig approach. *Econometrica 52 No. 2*, 449–460.

Hamilton, J. D. (1994). *Time Series Analysis*. Princeton: Princeton University Press.

Hansen, B. E. (1992). Tests for parameter instability in regressions with I(1) processes. *Journal of Business & Economic Statistics 10*, 321–335.

Hargreaves, H. S. P. (1980). Choosing the wrong 'natural' rate: Accelerating inflation or decelerating employment and growth? *Economic Journal 90*, 611–620.

Harsanyi, J. C. (1956). Approaches to the bargaining problem before and after the theory of games: A critical discussion of Zeuthen's, Hicks', and Nash's theories. *Econometrica 24*, 144–157.

Haug, A. A. (1996). Tests for cointegration: A Monte Carlo comparison. *Journal of Econometrics 71*, 89–115.

Hecq, A. and B. Mahy (1997). Testing for the price- and wage-setting model in Belgium using multivariate cointegration tests. *Labour 11(1)*, 177–199.

Hendry, D. F. (1995). *Dynamic Econometrics*. Oxford: Oxford University Press.

Holmlund, B. (1989). Wages and employment in unionized economies: Theory and evidence. In B. Holmlund, K.-G. Löfgren, and L. Engström (Eds.), *Trade Unions, Employment, and Unemployment Duration*, Oxford, pp. 5–131. Clarendon Press.

Hylleberg, S. (1995). Tests for seasonal unit roots: General to specific or specific to general? *Journal of Econometrics 69*, 5–25.

Hylleberg, S., R. F. Engle, C. W. J. Granger, and B. S. Yoo (1990). Seasonal integration and cointegration. *Journal of Econometrics 44*, 215–238.

Institut der deutschen Wirtschaft Köln (1996). Zahlen zur wirtschaftlichen Entwicklung der Bundesrepublik Deutschland.

Jaeger, A. and M. Parkinson (1994). Some evidence on hysteresis in unemployment rates. *European Economic Review 38*, 329–342.

Johansen, S. (1988). Statistical analysis of cointegration vectors. *Journal of Economic Dynamics and Control 12*, 231–254.

Johansen, S. (1992). Cointegration in partial systems and the efficency of single-equation analysis. *Journal of Econometrics 52*, 389–402.

Johansen, S. (1995). *Likelihood-Based Inference in Cointegrated Vector Autoregressive Models*. Oxford: Oxford University Press.

Kalai, E. (1977). Proportional solutions to bargaining situations: Interpersonel utility comparisons. *Econometrica 45(7)*, 1623–1630.

Kalai, E. and M. Smorodinsky (1975). Other solutions to Nash's bargaining problem. *Econometrica 43*, 513–518.

Koskela, E. and R. Schöb (1998). Why governments should tax mobile capital in the presence of unemployment. Working Paper 175, CES, University of Munich.

Krämer, W., W. Ploberger, and R. Alt (1988). Testing for structural change in dynamic models. *Econometrica 56*, 1355–1369.

Krasnosel'skii, M. A. and A. V. Pokrovskii (1989). *Systems with Hysteresis*. Berlin: Springer.

Kwiatkowski, D., P. C. B. Phillips, P. Schmidt, and Y. Shin (1992). Testing the null hypothesis of stationarity against the alternative of a unit root: How sure are we that economic time series have a unit root? *Journal of Econometrics 54*, 159–178.

Lahiri, K. and M. Nlandu (1995). Testing for cointegration: Power versus frequency of observation-another view. *Economics Letters 49*, 121–124.

Lee, H. S. (1992). Maximum likelihood inference on cointegration and seasonal cointegration. *Journal of Econometrics 54*, 1–47.

Lee, H. S. and P. L. Siklos (1995). A note on the critical values for the maximum likelihood (seasonal) cointegration tests. *Economics Letters 49*, 137–145.

Leontief, W. (1946). The pure theory of the guaranteed annual wage contract. *Journal of Political Economy 54*, 76–79.

Lever, M. H. (1995). Insider-outsider effects in wage formation: An empirical survey. *Bulletin of Economic Research 47:4*, 257–274.

Lindbeck, A. and D. J. Snower (1986a). Wage rigidity, union activity and unemployment. In W. Beckerman (Ed.), *Wage Rigidity & Unemployment*, London, pp. 97–126. Duckworth.

Lindbeck, A. and D. J. Snower (1986b). Wage setting, unemployment, and insider-outsider relations. *AEA Papers and Proceedings 76*, 235–239.

Lindbeck, A. and D. J. Snower (1988). Cooperation, harassment, and involuntary unemployment: An insider-outsider approach. *American Economic Review 78*, 167–188.

Machin, S. and J. Van Reenen (1998). Technology and changes in skill structure: Evidence from seven OECD countries. *Quartely Journal of Economics 113*, 1215–1244.

MacKinnon, J. G. (1994). Approximate asymptotic distribution functions for unit-root and cointegration tests. *Journal of Business & Economics Staistics 12*, 167–176.

Manning, A. (1993). Wage bargaining and the Phillips curve: The identification and specification of aggregate wage equations. *Economic Journal 103*, 98–118.

Manning, A. (1994). How robust is the microeconomic theory of the trade union? *Journal of Labor Economics 12(3)*, 430–459.

Manning, A. (1995a). Developments in labour market theory and their implications for macroeconomic policy. *Scottish Journal of Political Economy 42*, 250–266.

Manning, A. (1995b). How do we know that real wages are too high? *The Quarterly Journal of Economics 110*, 1111–1125.

Manzini, P. (1998). Game theoretic models of wage bargaining. *Journal of Economic Surveys 12*, 1–41.

Mayergoyz, I. (1991). *Mathematical Models of Hysteresis.* Berlin: Springer.

McDonald, I. M. and R. M. Solow (1981). Wage bargaining and employment. *American Economic Review 71*, 896–908.

Mizon, G. and J.-F. Richard (1986). The encompassing pinciple and its application to testing non-nested hypotheses. *Econometrica 54*, 657–678.

Mocan, N. H. and T. Kudret (1993). Real wages over the business cycle: Evidence from a structural time series model. *Oxford Bulletin of Economics and Statistics 55*, 363–389.

Nash, J. F. (1950). The bargaining problem. *Econometrica 18*, 155–162.

Nash, J. F. (1953). Two person cooperative games. *Econometrica 21*, 128–140.

Neftci, S. N. (1978). A time-series analysis of the real wages-employment relationship. *Journal of Political Economy 86*, 281–291.

Nelson, C. R. and C. I. Plosser (1982). Trends and random walks in macroeconomic time series. *Journal of Monetary Economics 10*, 139–162.

Newey, W. K. and K. D. West (1987). A simple, positive semi-definite, heteroskedasticity and autocorrelation consistent covariance matrix. *Econometrica 55*, 703–708.

Nickell, S. (1990). Unemployment: A survey. *Economic Journal 100*, 391–439.

Nickell, S. J. and M. Andrews (1983). Unions, real wages and employment in Britain 1951-79. *Oxford Economic Papers 35*, 183–206.

Nydegger, R. V. and G. Owen (1975). Two-person bargaining: An experimental test of the Nash axioms. *International Journal of Game Theory 3*, 239–249.

Oswald, A. J. (1985). The economic theory of trade unions: An introductory survey. *Scandinavian Journal of Economics 87(2)*, 160–193.

Park, J. Y. and P. C. B. Phillips (1988). Statistical inference in regressions with integrated processes: Part 1. *Econometric Theory 4*, 468–497.

Park, J. Y. and P. C. B. Phillips (1989). Statistical inference in regressions with integrated processes: Part 2. *Econometric Theory 5*, 95–131.

Pen, J. (1959). *The Wage Rate Under Collective Bargaining.* Cambridge, Mass.: Harvard University Press.

Perry, G. L. (1966). *Unemployment, Money Wage Rates, and Inflation.* Cambridge, Mass.: MIT Press.

Peters, H. J. M. (1992). *Axiomatic Bargaining Game Theory.* Dordrecht: Kluwer.

Phelps, E. S. (1994). *Structural Slumps.* Cambridge, Mass.: Harvard University Press.

Phillips, A. W. (1958). The relation between unemployment and the rate of change of money wage rates in the United Kingdom, 1861-1957. *Economica 25*, 283–299.

Phillips, P. C. B. (1986). Understanding spurious regressions in econometrics. *Journal of Econometrics 33*, 311–340.

Phillips, P. C. B. (1991). Optimal inference in cointegrated systems. *Econometrica 59*, 283–306.

Phillips, P. C. B. and S. N. Durlauf (1986). Multiple time series regression with integrated processes. *Review of Economic Studies 53*, 473–495.

Phillips, P. C. B. and B. E. Hansen (1990). Statistical inference in instrumental variables regression with I(1) processes. *Review of Economic Studies 57*, 99–125.

Phillips, P. C. B. and M. Loretan (1991). Estimating long-run economic equilibria. *Review of Economic Studies 58*, 407–436.

Phillips, P. C. B. and S. Ouliaris (1990). Asymptotic properties of residual based tests for cointegration. *Econometrica 58*, 165–193.

Popper, K. R. (1972). *Objective Knowledge: An Evolutionary Approach.* Oxford: Clarendon Press.

Profit, S. and R. Tschernig (1998). Germany's labor market problems: What to do and what not to do? *ifo Studien 44*, 307–326. SFB 373 Discussion Paper 94, Humboldt University Berlin.

Røed, K. (1997). Hysteresis in unemployment. *Journal of Economic Surveys 11*, 389–418.

Ross, A. M. (1948). *Trade Union Wage Policy.* Berkeley: UC Press.

Roth, A. E. (1979). *Axiomatic Models of Bargaining.* Berlin, Heidelberg, New York: Springer.

Roth, A. E. and M. W. K. Malouf (1979). Game-theoretic models and the role of information in bargaining. *Psychological Review 86*, 574–594.

Saikkonen, P. (1991). Asymptotically efficient estimation of cointegration regressions. *Econometric Theory 7*, 1–21.

Salop, S. C. (1979). A model of the natural rate of unemployment. *American Economic Review 69*, 117–125.

Schnabel, C. (1994). *Die Übertarifliche Bezahlung: Ausmaß, Entwicklung und Bestimmungsgründe.* Köln: Deutscher Instituts-Verlag GmbH.

Schnabel, R. (1998). Rates of return of the German pay-as-you-go pension system. *Finanzarchiv 55*, 374–399.

Shapiro, C. and J. E. Stiglitz (1984). Equilibrium unemployment as a worker discipline device. *American Economic Review 74*, 433–444.

Shiller, R. J. and P. Perron (1985). Testing the random walk hypothesis. *Economics Letters 18*, 381–386.

Sinn, H.-W. (1997). Deutschland im Steuerwettberwerb. *Jahrbücher für Nationalökonomie und Statistik 216/6*, 672–692.

Solon, G., R. Barsky, and J. A. Parker (1994). Measuring the cyclicality of real wages: How important is composition bias? *The Quarterly Journal of Economics 109*, 1–25.

Solow, R. M. (1979). Another possible source of wage stickiness. *Journal of Macroeconomics 1*, 79–82.

Solow, R. M. (1985). Insiders and outsiders in wage determination. *Scandinavian Journal of Economics 87*, 411–428.

Stiglitz, J. E. (1974). Alternative theories of wage determination and unemployment in LDC's: The labor turnover model. *Quarterly Journal of Economics 88*, 194–227.

Stock, J. H. and M. W. Watson (1988). Testing for common trends. *Journal of the American Statistical Association 83*, 1097–1107.

Sumner, S. and S. Silver (1989). Real wages, employment, and the Phillips curve. *Journal of Political Economy 97*, 706–720.

Tarshis, L. (1939). Changes in real and money wage rates. *Economic Journal 49*, 150–154.

Toda, H. Y. and P. C. B. Phillips (1993). Vector autoregression and causality. *Econometrica 61*, 1367–1393.

Tyrväinen, T. (1992). Unions, wages and employment: Evidence from Finland. *Applied Economics 24*, 1275–1286.

Tyrväinen, T. (1995a). Real wage resistance and unemployment: Multivariate analysis of cointegrating relations in 10 OECD countries. OECD Jobs Study, Working paper no. 10. Paris: OECD.

Tyrväinen, T. (1995b). Wage setting, taxes and demand for labour: Multivariate analysis of cointegrating relations. *Empirical Economics 20*, 271–297.

Urbain, J.-P. (1993). *Exogeneity in Error Correction Models.* Berlin: Springer.

Van der Ploeg, F. (1987). Trade unions, investment, and employment. *European Economic Review 31*, 1465–1492.

Weiss, A. (1980). Job queues and layoffs in labor markets with flexible wages. *Journal of Political Economy 88*, 526–538.

Weiss, A. (1991). *Efficiency Wages: Models of Unemployment, Layoffs and Wage Dispersion.* Oxford: Clarendon Press.

Wissenschaftlicher Beirat beim Bundesministerium für Wirtschaft (1998). *Grundlegende Reform der gesetzlichen Rentenversicherung.* Bonn: Bundesministerium für Wirtschaft.

Wolters, J. (1992). Persistence and seasonality in output and employment of the Federal Republic of Germany. *Recherches Economiques de Louvain 58*, 421–439.

Yule, G. U. (1926). Why do we sometimes get nonsense-correlations between time-series? A study in sampling and the nature of time series (with discussion). *Journal of the Royal Statistical Society 89*, 1–64.

Zeuthen, F. (1930). *Problems of Monopoly and Economic Warfare*. London: Routledge.

Lecture Notes in Economics and Mathematical Systems

For information about Vols. 1–305
please contact your bookseller or Springer-Verlag

Vol. 306: Ch. Klein, A Static Microeconomic Model of Pure Competition. VIII, 139 pages. 1988.

Vol. 307: T.K. Dijkstra (Ed.), On Model Uncertainty and its Statistical Implications. VII, 138 pages. 1988.

Vol. 308: J.R. Daduna, A. Wren (Eds.), Computer-Aided Transit Scheduling. VIII, 339 pages. 1988.

Vol. 309: G. Ricci, K. Velupillai (Eds.), Growth Cycles and Multisectoral Economics: The Goodwin Tradition. III, 126 pages. 1988.

Vol. 310: J. Kacprzyk, M. Fedrizzi (Eds.), Combining Fuzzy Imprecision with Probabilistic Uncertainty in Decision Making. IX, 399 pages. 1988.

Vol. 311: R. Färe, Fundamentals of Production Theory. IX, 163 pages. 1988.

Vol. 312: J. Krishnakumar, Estimation of Simultaneous Equation Models with Error Components Structure. X, 357 pages. 1988.

Vol. 313: W. Jammernegg, Sequential Binary Investment Decisions. VI, 156 pages. 1988.

Vol. 314: R. Tietz, W. Albers, R. Selten (Eds.), Bounded Rational Behavior in Experimental Games and Markets. VI, 368 pages. 1988.

Vol. 315: I. Orishimo, G.J.D. Hewings, P. Nijkamp (Eds), Information Technology: Social and Spatial Perspectives. Proceedings 1986. VI, 268 pages. 1988.

Vol. 316: R.L. Basmann, D.J. Slottje, K. Hayes, J.D. Johnson, D.J. Molina, The Generalized Fechner-Thurstone Direct Utility Function and Some of its Uses. VIII, 159 pages. 1988.

Vol. 317: L. Bianco, A. La Bella (Eds.), Freight Transport Planning and Logistics. Proceedings, 1987. X, 568 pages. 1988.

Vol. 318: T. Doup, Simplicial Algorithms on the Simplotope. VIII, 262 pages. 1988.

Vol. 319: D.T. Luc, Theory of Vector Optimization. VIII, 173 pages. 1989.

Vol. 320: D. van der Wijst, Financial Structure in Small Business. VII, 181 pages. 1989.

Vol. 321: M. Di Matteo, R.M. Goodwin, A. Vercelli (Eds.), Technological and Social Factors in Long Term Fluctuations. Proceedings. IX, 442 pages. 1989.

Vol. 322: T. Kollintzas (Ed.), The Rational Expectations Equilibrium Inventory Model. XI, 269 pages. 1989.

Vol. 323: M.B.M. de Koster, Capacity Oriented Analysis and Design of Production Systems. XII, 245 pages. 1989.

Vol. 324: I.M. Bomze, B.M. Pötscher, Game Theoretical Foundations of Evolutionary Stability. VI, 145 pages. 1989.

Vol. 325: P. Ferri, E. Greenberg, The Labor Market and Business Cycle Theories. X, 183 pages. 1989.

Vol. 326: Ch. Sauer, Alternative Theories of Output, Unemployment, and Inflation in Germany: 1960–1985. XIII, 206 pages. 1989.

Vol. 327: M. Tawada, Production Structure and International Trade. V, 132 pages. 1989.

Vol. 328: W. Güth, B. Kalkofen, Unique Solutions for Strategic Games. VII, 200 pages. 1989.

Vol. 329: G. Tillmann, Equity, Incentives, and Taxation. VI, 132 pages. 1989.

Vol. 330: P.M. Kort, Optimal Dynamic Investment Policies of a Value Maximizing Firm. VII, 185 pages. 1989.

Vol. 331: A. Lewandowski, A.P. Wierzbicki (Eds.), Aspiration Based Decision Support Systems. X, 400 pages. 1989.

Vol. 332: T.R. Gulledge, Jr., L.A. Litteral (Eds.), Cost Analysis Applications of Economics and Operations Research. Proceedings. VII, 422 pages. 1989.

Vol. 333: N. Dellaert, Production to Order. VII, 158 pages. 1989.

Vol. 334: H.-W. Lorenz, Nonlinear Dynamical Economics and Chaotic Motion. XI, 248 pages. 1989.

Vol. 335: A.G. Lockett, G. Islei (Eds.), Improving Decision Making in Organisations. Proceedings. IX, 606 pages. 1989.

Vol. 336: T. Puu, Nonlinear Economic Dynamics. VII, 119 pages. 1989.

Vol. 337: A. Lewandowski, I. Stanchev (Eds.), Methodology and Software for Interactive Decision Support. VIII, 309 pages. 1989.

Vol. 338: J.K. Ho, R.P. Sundarraj, DECOMP: An Implementation of Dantzig-Wolfe Decomposition for Linear Programming. VI, 206 pages.

Vol. 339: J. Terceiro Lomba, Estimation of Dynamic Econometric Models with Errors in Variables. VIII, 116 pages. 1990.

Vol. 340: T. Vasko, R. Ayres, L. Fontvieille (Eds.), Life Cycles and Long Waves. XIV, 293 pages. 1990.

Vol. 341: G.R. Uhlich, Descriptive Theories of Bargaining. IX, 165 pages. 1990.

Vol. 342: K. Okuguchi, F. Szidarovszky, The Theory of Oligopoly with Multi-Product Firms. V, 167 pages. 1990.

Vol. 343: C. Chiarella, The Elements of a Nonlinear Theory of Economic Dynamics. IX, 149 pages. 1990.

Vol. 344: K. Neumann, Stochastic Project Networks. XI, 237 pages. 1990.

Vol. 345: A. Cambini, E. Castagnoli, L. Martein, P Mazzoleni, S. Schaible (Eds.), Generalized Convexity and Fractional Programming with Economic Applications. Proceedings, 1988. VII, 361 pages. 1990.

Vol. 346: R. von Randow (Ed.), Integer Programming and Related Areas. A Classified Bibliography 1984–1987. XIII, 514 pages. 1990.

Vol. 347: D. Ríos Insua, Sensitivity Analysis in Multi-objective Decision Making. XI, 193 pages. 1990.

Vol. 348: H. Störmer, Binary Functions and their Applications. VIII, 151 pages. 1990.

Vol. 349: G.A. Pfann, Dynamic Modelling of Stochastic Demand for Manufacturing Employment. VI, 158 pages. 1990.

Vol. 350: W.-B. Zhang, Economic Dynamics. X, 232 pages. 1990.

Vol. 351: A. Lewandowski, V. Volkovich (Eds.), Multiobjective Problems of Mathematical Programming. Proceedings, 1988. VII, 315 pages. 1991.

Vol. 352: O. van Hilten, Optimal Firm Behaviour in the Context of Technological Progress and a Business Cycle. XII, 229 pages. 1991.

Vol. 353: G. Ricci (Ed.), Decision Processes in Economics. Proceedings, 1989. III, 209 pages 1991.

Vol. 354: M. Ivaldi, A Structural Analysis of Expectation Formation. XII, 230 pages. 1991.

Vol. 355: M. Salomon. Deterministic Lotsizing Models for Production Planning. VII, 158 pages. 1991.

Vol. 356: P. Korhonen, A. Lewandowski, J . Wallenius (Eds.), Multiple Criteria Decision Support. Proceedings, 1989. XII, 393 pages. 1991.

Vol. 357: P. Zörnig, Degeneracy Graphs and Simplex Cycling. XV, 194 pages. 1991.

Vol. 358: P. Knottnerus, Linear Models with Correlated Disturbances. VIII, 196 pages. 1991.

Vol. 359: E. de Jong, Exchange Rate Determination and Optimal Economic Policy Under Various Exchange Rate Regimes. VII, 270 pages. 1991.

Vol. 360: P. Stalder, Regime Translations, Spillovers and Buffer Stocks. VI, 193 pages . 1991.

Vol. 361: C. F. Daganzo, Logistics Systems Analysis. X, 321 pages. 1991.

Vol. 362: F. Gehrels, Essays in Macroeconomics of an Open Economy. VII, 183 pages. 1991.

Vol. 363: C. Puppe, Distorted Probabilities and Choice under Risk. VIII, 100 pages . 1991

Vol. 364: B. Horvath, Are Policy Variables Exogenous? XII, 162 pages. 1991.

Vol. 365: G. A. Heuer, U. Leopold-Wildburger. Balanced Silverman Games on General Discrete Sets. V, 140 pages. 1991.

Vol. 366: J. Gruber (Ed.), Econometric Decision Models. Proceedings, 1989. VIII, 636 pages. 1991.

Vol. 367: M. Grauer, D. B. Pressmar (Eds.), Parallel Computing and Mathematical Optimization. Proceedings. V, 208 pages. 1991.

Vol. 368: M. Fedrizzi, J. Kacprzyk, M. Roubens (Eds.), Interactive Fuzzy Optimization. VII, 216 pages. 1991.

Vol. 369: R. Koblo, The Visible Hand. VIII, 131 pages.1991.

Vol. 370: M. J. Beckmann, M. N. Gopalan, R. Subramanian (Eds.), Stochastic Processes and their Applications. Proceedings, 1990. XLI, 292 pages. 1991.

Vol. 371: A. Schmutzler, Flexibility and Adjustment to Information in Sequential Decision Problems. VIII, 198 pages. 1991.

Vol. 372: J. Esteban, The Social Viability of Money. X, 202 pages. 1991.

Vol. 373: A. Billot, Economic Theory of Fuzzy Equilibria. XIII, 164 pages. 1992.

Vol. 374: G. Pflug, U. Dieter (Eds.), Simulation and Optimization. Proceedings, 1990. X, 162 pages. 1992.

Vol. 375: S.-J. Chen, Ch.-L. Hwang, Fuzzy Multiple Attribute Decision Making. XII, 536 pages. 1992.

Vol. 376: K.-H. Jöckel, G. Rothe, W. Sendler (Eds.), Bootstrapping and Related Techniques. Proceedings, 1990. VIII, 247 pages. 1992.

Vol. 377: A. Villar, Operator Theorems with Applications to Distributive Problems and Equilibrium Models. XVI, 160 pages. 1992.

Vol. 378: W. Krabs, J. Zowe (Eds.), Modern Methods of Optimization. Proceedings, 1990. VIII, 348 pages. 1992.

Vol. 379: K. Marti (Ed.), Stochastic Optimization. Proceedings, 1990. VII, 182 pages. 1992.

Vol. 380: J. Odelstad, Invariance and Structural Dependence. XII, 245 pages. 1992.

Vol. 381: C. Giannini, Topics in Structural VAR Econometrics. XI, 131 pages. 1992.

Vol. 382: W. Oettli, D. Pallaschke (Eds.), Advances in Optimization. Proceedings, 1991. X, 527 pages. 1992.

Vol. 383: J. Vartiainen, Capital Accumulation in a Corporatist Economy. VII, 177 pages. 1992.

Vol. 384: A. Martina, Lectures on the Economic Theory of Taxation. XII, 313 pages. 1992.

Vol. 385: J. Gardeazabal, M. Regúlez, The Monetary Model of Exchange Rates and Cointegration. X, 194 pages. 1992.

Vol. 386: M. Desrochers, J.-M. Rousseau (Eds.), Computer-Aided Transit Scheduling. Proceedings, 1990. XIII, 432 pages. 1992.

Vol. 387: W. Gaertner, M. Klemisch-Ahlert, Social Choice and Bargaining Perspectives on Distributive Justice. VIII, 131 pages. 1992.

Vol. 388: D. Bartmann, M. J. Beckmann, Inventory Control. XV, 252 pages. 1992.

Vol. 389: B. Dutta, D. Mookherjee, T. Parthasarathy, T. Raghavan, D. Ray, S. Tijs (Eds.), Game Theory and Economic Applications. Proceedings, 1990. IX, 454 pages. 1992.

Vol. 390: G. Sorger, Minimum Impatience Theorem for Recursive Economic Models. X, 162 pages. 1992.

Vol. 391: C. Keser, Experimental Duopoly Markets with Demand Inertia. X, 150 pages. 1992.

Vol. 392: K. Frauendorfer, Stochastic Two-Stage Programming. VIII, 228 pages. 1992.

Vol. 393: B. Lucke, Price Stabilization on World Agricultural Markets. XI, 274 pages. 1992.

Vol. 394: Y.-J. Lai, C.-L. Hwang, Fuzzy Mathematical Programming. XIII, 301 pages. 1992.

Vol. 395: G. Haag, U. Mueller, K. G. Troitzsch (Eds.), Economic Evolution and Demographic Change. XVI, 409 pages. 1992.

Vol. 396: R. V. V. Vidal (Ed.), Applied Simulated Annealing. VIII, 358 pages. 1992.

Vol. 397: J. Wessels, A. P. Wierzbicki (Eds.), User-Oriented Methodology and Techniques of Decision Analysis and Support. Proceedings, 1991. XII, 295 pages. 1993.

Vol. 398: J.-P. Urbain, Exogeneity in Error Correction Models. XI, 189 pages. 1993.

Vol. 399: F. Gori, L. Geronazzo, M. Galeotti (Eds.), Nonlinear Dynamics in Economics and Social Sciences. Proceedings, 1991. VIII, 367 pages. 1993.

Vol. 400: H. Tanizaki, Nonlinear Filters. XII, 203 pages. 1993.

Vol. 401: K. Mosler, M. Scarsini, Stochastic Orders and Applications. V, 379 pages. 1993.

Vol. 402: A. van den Elzen, Adjustment Processes for Exchange Economies and Noncooperative Games. VII, 146 pages. 1993.

Vol. 403: G. Brennscheidt, Predictive Behavior. VI, 227 pages. 1993.

Vol. 404: Y.-J. Lai, Ch.-L. Hwang, Fuzzy Multiple Objective Decision Making. XIV, 475 pages. 1994.

Vol. 405: S. Komlósi, T. Rapcsák, S. Schaible (Eds.), Generalized Convexity. Proceedings, 1992. VIII, 404 pages. 1994.

Vol. 406: N. M. Hung, N. V. Quyen, Dynamic Timing Decisions Under Uncertainty. X, 194 pages. 1994.

Vol. 407: M. Ooms, Empirical Vector Autoregressive Modeling. XIII, 380 pages. 1994.

Vol. 408: K. Haase, Lotsizing and Scheduling for Production Planning. VIII, 118 pages. 1994.

Vol. 409: A. Sprecher, Resource-Constrained Project Scheduling. XII, 142 pages. 1994.

Vol. 410: R. Winkelmann, Count Data Models. XI, 213 pages. 1994.

Vol. 411: S. Dauzère-Péres, J.-B. Lasserre, An Integrated Approach in Production Planning and Scheduling. XVI, 137 pages. 1994.

Vol. 412: B. Kuon, Two-Person Bargaining Experiments with Incomplete Information. IX, 293 pages. 1994.

Vol. 413: R. Fiorito (Ed.), Inventory, Business Cycles and Monetary Transmission. VI, 287 pages. 1994.

Vol. 414: Y. Crama, A. Oerlemans, F. Spieksma, Production Planning in Automated Manufacturing. X, 210 pages. 1994.

Vol. 415: P. C. Nicola, Imperfect General Equilibrium. XI, 167 pages. 1994.

Vol. 416: H. S. J. Cesar, Control and Game Models of the Greenhouse Effect. XI, 225 pages. 1994.

Vol. 417: B. Ran, D. E. Boyce, Dynamic Urban Transportation Network Models. XV, 391 pages. 1994.

Vol. 418: P. Bogetoft, Non-Cooperative Planning Theory. XI, 309 pages. 1994.

Vol. 419: T. Maruyama, W. Takahashi (Eds.), Nonlinear and Convex Analysis in Economic Theory. VIII, 306 pages. 1995.

Vol. 420: M. Peeters, Time-To-Build. Interrelated Investment and Labour Demand Modelling. With Applications to Six OECD Countries. IX, 204 pages. 1995.

Vol. 421: C. Dang, Triangulations and Simplicial Methods. IX, 196 pages. 1995.

Vol. 422: D. S. Bridges, G. B. Mehta, Representations of Preference Orderings. X, 165 pages. 1995.

Vol. 423: K. Marti, P. Kall (Eds.), Stochastic Programming. Numerical Techniques and Engineering Applications. VIII, 351 pages. 1995.

Vol. 424: G. A. Heuer, U. Leopold-Wildburger, Silverman's Game. X, 283 pages. 1995.

Vol. 425: J. Kohlas, P.-A. Monney, A Mathematical Theory of Hints. XIII, 419 pages, 1995.

Vol. 426: B. Finkenstädt, Nonlinear Dynamics in Economics. IX, 156 pages. 1995.

Vol. 427: F. W. van Tongeren, Microsimulation Modelling of the Corporate Firm. XVII, 275 pages. 1995.

Vol. 428: A. A. Powell, Ch. W. Murphy, Inside a Modern Macroeconometric Model. XVIII, 424 pages. 1995.

Vol. 429: R. Durier, C. Michelot, Recent Developments in Optimization. VIII, 356 pages. 1995.

Vol. 430: J. R. Daduna, I. Branco, J. M. Pinto Paixão (Eds.), Computer-Aided Transit Scheduling. XIV, 374 pages. 1995.

Vol. 431: A. Aulin, Causal and Stochastic Elements in Business Cycles. XI, 116 pages. 1996.

Vol. 432: M. Tamiz (Ed.), Multi-Objective Programming and Goal Programming. VI, 359 pages. 1996.

Vol. 433: J. Menon, Exchange Rates and Prices. XIV, 313 pages. 1996.

Vol. 434: M. W. J. Blok, Dynamic Models of the Firm. VII, 193 pages. 1996.

Vol. 435: L. Chen, Interest Rate Dynamics, Derivatives Pricing, and Risk Management. XII, 149 pages. 1996.

Vol. 436: M. Klemisch-Ahlert, Bargaining in Economic and Ethical Environments. IX, 155 pages. 1996.

Vol. 437: C. Jordan, Batching and Scheduling. IX, 178 pages. 1996.

Vol. 438: A. Villar, General Equilibrium with Increasing Returns. XIII, 164 pages. 1996.

Vol. 439: M. Zenner, Learning to Become Rational. VII, 201 pages. 1996.

Vol. 440: W. Ryll, Litigation and Settlement in a Game with Incomplete Information. VIII, 174 pages. 1996.

Vol. 441: H. Dawid, Adaptive Learning by Genetic Algorithms. IX, 166 pages.1996.

Vol. 442: L. Corchón, Theories of Imperfectly Competitive Markets. XIII, 163 pages. 1996.

Vol. 443: G. Lang, On Overlapping Generations Models with Productive Capital. X, 98 pages. 1996.

Vol. 444: S. Jørgensen, G. Zaccour (Eds.), Dynamic Competitive Analysis in Marketing. X, 285 pages. 1996.

Vol. 445: A. H. Christer, S. Osaki, L. C. Thomas (Eds.), Stochastic Modelling in Innovative Manufactoring. X, 361 pages. 1997.

Vol. 446: G. Dhaene, Encompassing. X, 160 pages. 1997.

Vol. 447: A. Artale, Rings in Auctions. X, 172 pages. 1997.

Vol. 448: G. Fandel, T. Gal (Eds.), Multiple Criteria Decision Making. XII, 678 pages. 1997.

Vol. 449: F. Fang, M. Sanglier (Eds.), Complexity and Self-Organization in Social and Economic Systems. IX, 317 pages, 1997.

Vol. 450: P. M. Pardalos, D. W. Hearn, W. W. Hager, (Eds.), Network Optimization. VIII, 485 pages, 1997.

Vol. 451: M. Salge, Rational Bubbles. Theoretical Basis, Economic Relevance, and Empirical Evidence with a Special Emphasis on the German Stock Market.IX, 265 pages. 1997.

Vol. 452: P. Gritzmann, R. Horst, E. Sachs, R. Tichatschke (Eds.), Recent Advances in Optimization. VIII, 379 pages. 1997.

Vol. 453: A. S. Tangian, J. Gruber (Eds.), Constructing Scalar-Valued Objective Functions. VIII, 298 pages. 1997.

Vol. 454: H.-M. Krolzig, Markov-Switching Vector Autoregressions. XIV, 358 pages. 1997.

Vol. 455: R. Caballero, F. Ruiz, R. E. Steuer (Eds.), Advances in Multiple Objective and Goal Programming. VIII, 391 pages. 1997.

Vol. 456: R. Conte, R. Hegselmann, P. Terna (Eds.), Simulating Social Phenomena. VIII, 536 pages. 1997.

Vol. 457: C. Hsu, Volume and the Nonlinear Dynamics of Stock Returns. VIII, 133 pages. 1998.

Vol. 458: K. Marti, P. Kall (Eds.), Stochastic Programming Methods and Technical Applications. X, 437 pages. 1998.

Vol. 459: H. K. Ryu, D. J. Slottje, Measuring Trends in U.S. Income Inequality. XI, 195 pages. 1998.

Vol. 460: B. Fleischmann, J. A. E. E. van Nunen, M. G. Speranza, P. Stähly, Advances in Distribution Logistic. XI, 535 pages. 1998.

Vol. 461: U. Schmidt, Axiomatic Utility Theory under Risk. XV, 201 pages. 1998.

Vol. 462: L. von Auer, Dynamic Preferences, Choice Mechanisms, and Welfare. XII, 226 pages. 1998.

Vol. 463: G. Abraham-Frois (Ed.), Non-Linear Dynamics and Endogenous Cycles. VI, 204 pages. 1998.

Vol. 464: A. Aulin, The Impact of Science on Economic Growth and its Cycles. IX, 204 pages. 1998.

Vol. 465: T. J. Stewart, R. C. van den Honert (Eds.), Trends in Multicriteria Decision Making. X, 448 pages. 1998.

Vol. 466: A. Sadrieh, The Alternating Double Auction Market. VII, 350 pages. 1998.

Vol. 467: H. Hennig-Schmidt, Bargaining in a Video Experiment. Determinants of Boundedly Rational Behavior. XII, 221 pages. 1999.

Vol. 468: A. Ziegler, A Game Theory Analysis of Options. XIV, 145 pages. 1999.

Vol. 469: M. P. Vogel, Environmental Kuznets Curves. XIII, 197 pages. 1999.

Vol. 470: M. Ammann, Pricing Derivative Credit Risk. XII, 228 pages. 1999.

Vol. 471: N. H. M. Wilson (Ed.), Computer-Aided Transit Scheduling. XI, 444 pages. 1999.

Vol. 472: J.-R. Tyran, Money Illusion and Strategic Complementarity as Causes of Monetary Non-Neutrality. X, 228 pages. 1999.

Vol. 473: S. Helber, Performance Analysis of Flow Lines with Non-Linear Flow of Material. IX, 280 pages. 1999.

Vol. 474: U. Schwalbe, The Core of Economies with Asymmetric Information. IX, 141 pages. 1999.

Vol. 475: L. Kaas, Dynamic Macroeconomics with Imperfect Competition. XI, 155 pages. 1999.

Vol. 476: R. Demel, Fiscal Policy, Public Debt and the Term Structure of Interest Rates. X, 279 pages. 1999.

Vol. 477: M. Théra, R. Tichatschke (Eds.), Ill-posed Variational Problems and Regularization Techniques. VIII, 274 pages. 1999.

Vol. 478: S. Hartmann, Project Scheduling under Limited Resources. XII, 221 pages. 1999.

Vol. 479: L. v. Thadden, Money, Inflation, and Capital Formation. IX, 192 pages. 1999.

Vol. 480: M. Grazia Speranza, P. Stähly (Eds.), New Trends in Distribution Logistics. X, 336 pages. 1999.

Vol. 481: V. H. Nguyen, J. J. Strodiot, P. Tossings (Eds.). Optimation. IX, 498 pages. 2000.

Vol. 482: W. B. Zhang, A Theory of International Trade. XI, 192 pages. 2000.

Vol. 483: M. Königstein, Equity, Efficiency and Evolutionary Stability in Bargaining Games with Joint Production. XII, 197 pages. 2000.

Vol. 484: D. D. Gatti, M. Gallegati, A. Kirman, Interaction and Market Structure. VI, 298 pages. 2000.

Vol. 485: A. Garnaev, Search Games and Other Applications of Game Theory. VIII, 145 pages. 2000.

Vol. 486: M. Neugart, Nonlinear Labor Market Dynamics. X, 175 pages. 2000.

Vol. 487: Y. Y. Haimes, R. E. Steuer (Eds.), Research and Practice in Multiple Criteria Decision Making. XVII, 553 pages. 2000.

Vol. 488: B. Schmolck, Ommitted Variable Tests and Dynamic Specification. X, 144 pages. 2000.

Vol. 489: T. Steger, Transitional Dynamics and Economic Growth in Developing Countries. VIII, 151 pages. 2000.

Vol. 490: S. Minner, Strategic Safety Stocks in Supply Chains. XI, 214 pages. 2000.

Vol. 491: M. Ehrgott, Multicriteria Optimization. VIII, 242 pages. 2000.

Vol. 492: T. Phan Huy, Constraint Propagation in Flexible Manufacturing. IX, 258 pages. 2000.

Vol. 493: J. Zhu, Modular Pricing of Options. X, 170 pages. 2000.

Vol. 494: D. Franzen, Design of Master Agreements for OTC Derivatives. VIII, 175 pages. 2001.

Vol. 495: I Konnov, Combined Relaxation Methods for Variational Inequalities. XI, 181 pages. 2001.

Vol. 496: P. Weiß, Unemployment in Open Economies. XII, 226 pages. 2001.

Vol. 497: J. Inkmann, Conditional Moment Estimation of Nonlinear Equation Systems. VIII, 214 pages. 2001.

Vol. 498: M. Reutter, A Macroeconomic Model of West German Unemployment. X, 125 pages. 2001.

Batch number: 10844675

Printed by Printforce, the Netherlands